The Vidstrom Labs Guide to

Arduino Assembly Language Programming

by Arne Vidstrom

Arduino Assembly Language Programming

Copyright © 2019 by Arne Vidstrom

Published by Vidstrom Labs, Karlstad, Sweden
https://vidstromlabs.com

Cover and Interior Illustration by Anna Vidstrom
https://vidstromillustration.com

International Standard Book Number: 978-91-985661-0-9

2 3 4 5 6 7 8 9 10

No part of this book may be reprinted, reproduced, transmitted, or stored in any information storage system, in any form or by any means, electronic or mechanical, including photocopying, scanning, microfilming, and audio recording, without prior written permission from the copyright owner.

This book is provided on an "As-Is" basis, without warranty of any kind, express or implied. In no event shall the copyright holder or publisher be liable for any claim, damages, or other liability.

Contents

Chapter 1. Introduction — 1
    What You Already Need to Know — 1
    The Hardware You Need — 2
    The Source Code, Errata, and Links — 2

Chapter 2. Machine Code and Assembly Language — 3
    An Introduction to Machine Code — 3
    From Machine Code to Assembly Language — 5
    Why Learning Assembly Language Is Useful Even If You Already Know C/C++ — 6

Chapter 3. The 8-bit AVR Architecture — 9

Chapter 4. Assembly Code in Sketches — 13
    Understanding the asm Statement — 14
    Clobbered Call-Used Registers Must Be in the Clobber List Too — 17
    Never Rely on the Clobber List for r1 — 17
    Sometimes You Can Use Basic asm Statements — 19

Chapter 5. Hello World: Blinking the Debug LED — 21
    Calling the delay() Function from Assembly Code — 22
    Blinking the Debug LED Through the Data Space — 23
    Blinking the Debug LED Through the I/O Space — 24
    Blinking the Debug LED With More Precision — 26

Chapter 6. Constraints — 29
    How to Choose Constraints — 30
    Using Constants Instead of Magic Numbers — 30
    Passing Input Operands Longer Than One Byte — 32

Chapter 7. A Closer Look at How Instructions Work — 35
    Understanding the AVR Assembly Documentation — 36
    What It Looks Like in Machine Code — 37
    The Status Register — 38
    An SREG Flag Example: The Carry Flag — 40

Chapter 8. The Pointer Register Pairs — 43
    Using a Pointer Register Pair — 43
    Pointer Register Pairs and Constraints — 45

Chapter 9. Basic Jumping and Branching — 47
Relative Jumps — 48
Branching Instructions — 49
The Importance of Picking the Correct Constraint — 51

Chapter 10. The Stack — 53
The Stack Pointer — 55
Push and Pop — 57
Function Arguments and the Stack — 58
Function Return Addresses and the Stack — 61

Chapter 11. Functions — 65
Pure Assembly Functions Called From C/C++ Code — 66
When a C/C++ Function Calls Another C/C++ Function — 69
When a C/C++ Function Contains an Extended asm Statement, Part 1 — 76
Earlyclobber Operands — 77
When a C/C++ Function Contains an Extended asm Statement, Part 2 — 78
Call-Used and Call-Saved Registers — 80
A Repeated Warning About the Call-Used Registers — 81

Chapter 12. Logic, Shift and Rotate Instructions — 83
Logic Instructions — 83
Leftward Shift and Rotate Instructions — 84
Rightward Shift and Rotate Instructions — 86

Chapter 13. Interrupts — 87
Using Interrupts to Blink the Debug LED — 87
The Global Interrupt Flag — 91
A Warning About the Zero Register in Interrupt Handlers — 91
Macros for Interrupt Handlers — 92
Interrupt Vector Names — 93

Chapter 14. Assembly Files — 95

Chapter 15. Arithmetic and Logic Instructions — 99
Accessing Global Variables — 99
Incrementing and Decrementing — 100
Two's Complement — 100
Adding Signed and Unsigned Numbers — 102
Unsigned Carry and Signed Overflow — 104
Signed and Unsigned Addition with Carry — 107
Subtraction with and without Carry — 108

Arithmetic Shift Right	110
Unsigned and Signed Multiplication	114
Function Calling Conventions Revisited: Signed 8-bit Return Values	116

Chapter 16. More Jumping and Branching — 119
- A Simple Branch Example — 119
- A Loop Example — 121
- A Switch Example — 122
- A Branch Table Example — 125
- An Empty Sketch and a Delay Subroutine — 129

Chapter 17. Memory Clobbering — 133

Chapter 18. Assembly Files Revisited — 139
- Assembly Files and Preprocessing — 139
- Using Macro Substitutions — 139

Chapter 19. Inline Assembly or Assembly Files — 143

Appendix A. Disassembling a Compiled Sketch — 145
- On macOS — 145
- On Windows — 146

Appendix B. Where to Find More Information — 147

Index — 151

Chapter 1.
Introduction

What You Already Need to Know

To follow this book successfully, you need some previous Arduino programming experience in C/C++ with the Arduino IDE. I write "C/C++" throughout the book because I don't want to get into a long-winded discussion about what the "Arduino programming language" really is. You need a good grasp of the bitwise operators (&, |, ^, <<, and >>) and pointer programming in C/C++. I also assume that you're well acquainted with how decimal, binary, and hexadecimal numbers work and can convert them back and forth. A basic understanding of what interrupts and timers are from a C/C++ programmer's point of view is required to comprehend the chapter about interrupts.

The Hardware You Need

You can use either the Arduino Uno or the Arduino Mega 2560 with this book. You don't need any extra hardware or electronic components or wires. I only assume that you have an interest in assembly language—not necessarily an interest in electronics. That's why you only need the Arduino and nothing else to run the examples.

The Source Code, Errata, and Links

You can find the source code and errata for the book at:

`https://vidstromlabs.com/books/arduinoassembly/`

All the links from the book are there too, so you don't have to type them in.

Chapter 2.
Machine Code and Assembly Language

An Introduction to Machine Code

When you create a sketch in C/C++ and upload it, the compiler turns it into **machine code**, which is the only type of code that the CPU[1] in your Arduino understands. Machine code consists of a series of binary numbers, like these:

```
00001110
10010100
00001110
00000011
00001110
10010100
10010010
00000011
```

---

1   Perhaps you already know that the Arduino is based on a microcontroller. I'm talking about the CPU core that's inside that microcontroller.

The machine code is divided into **opcodes** (operation codes). Each opcode is a binary pattern that tells the CPU to perform a specific task, like adding two numbers or copying data from one location to another. The CPU **executes** the opcodes.

You can write entire programs in machine code, and the principles behind it aren't as hard to grasp as it might seem, but some aspects *are* hard. For example, you can't always write machine code from scratch using hexadecimal numbers. The opcode for the assembly instruction[2] called `brts` is an instance where it doesn't work. The bits 0 to 2 of the opcode have a different meaning than bit 3.[3] One hexadecimal digit represents four bits, so there's no easy way to handle these two different sets of bits using hexadecimal. It's not until you've determined what the opcode should look like in binary that you can convert it to hexadecimal.

You have to consult the documentation each time you encode an instruction unless you memorize sequences of opcode bits. That makes programming in machine code a slow and tedious process, because few people can memorize a large number of bit sequences with perfect recall. For the same reason, it's also nearly impossible to look at machine code and immediately understand what it does. You must use the documentation to decode it first, which makes reading machine code a slow and tedious process too.

Even worse, you have to keep track of memory addresses manually when you program in machine code. Here is some machine code in hexadecimal, with addresses on the left:

```
62e:    0e 94 65 01
632:    fd cf
```

The machine code at address 632 performs a jump back to address 62e, but that address isn't encoded in the opcode. Instead, the opcode makes a jump six bytes back, counted from the address of the next opcode following it. Since the jump opcode is two bytes long, the next opcode is at address 634, and 634 – 6 equals 62e.

---

2   Don't worry about what an assembly instruction is if you don't already know. I'll explain it later. Read on and see how painful it can be to program in machine code.
3   The least significant bit of a byte is called bit 0, and the most significant bit is called bit 7. For a 16-bit word, the corresponding bits are 0 and 15.

Imagine that you want to add another opcode between the two lines above, like this:

```
62e:    0e 94 65 01
632:    8c 0f
634:    fd cf
```

You still want to jump from the last line to the first line, but where do you land now? You land at address 634 + 2 − 6 = 630. That's in the middle of the opcode at address 62e. Your program will crash. To make this work, you must change the jump opcode at address 634. Imagine what it would be like with a program consisting of thousands of opcodes. Make one small change, and you may have to make several other changes. Some of those changes may necessitate even more changes, and so on. Enter assembly language.

From Machine Code to Assembly Language

Assembly language alleviates some of the pains associated with programming in machine code. In machine code, we had a problem with encoding the `brts` instruction straight into hexadecimal numbers. In assembly language, you write something like this:

```
brts yourlabel
    .
    .
    .
yourlabel:
```

Some of the bits of the opcode for `brts yourlabel` refer to the `brts` instruction itself and others refer to `yourlabel`. That's why we must write the opcode in binary first, and then convert it to hexadecimal. An opcode represents both an assembly language **instruction** and the specification of what it should operate on. You don't have to worry about any of that when you program in assembly language, because the correct machine code is generated automatically for you.

Target addresses that change aren't a problem either when you use **labels**, like `yourlabel`. If you add some new instructions, all existing labels still refer to the correct locations, and you don't have to recalculate anything at all.

Why Learning Assembly Language Is Useful Even If You Already Know C/C++

Nowadays, most developers never program in assembly language. Nearly all tasks can be accomplished using higher-level languages, but that doesn't make assembly language an esoteric hobby. Learning assembly language is fun, but it also helps you understand how things work under the hood.

When you learn assembly language, you also learn more about the hardware at the same time. C/C++ and various libraries abstract away many details. Abstractions are useful, but they're seldom perfect, and we're often left with what is called **leaky abstractions**. Learning assembly language can make you a more reliable C/C++ programmer because it makes you better equipped to handle these leaky abstractions.

Knowing assembly language can also help you write more efficient code. Modern compilers are very good at optimizing the machine code they generate, but they're not perfect. If you're good enough at it, you can occasionally beat the compiler if you write some of the code in assembly language. Beware, though: sometimes you might *think* that you're beating the compiler when you're actually writing *less* efficient code. Always measure the results of your optimizations to make sure that you really are optimizing!

Assembly language is also useful for **reverse engineering**. You can use a **disassembler** to **disassemble** compiled code into assembly language and then try to figure out how it works. That can be useful in several different ways. For example, it can help you understand how undocumented features work and how to interface with them. It can also help you find bugs in your code. Sometimes, looking at a disassembly of your compiled C/C++ code will help you troubleshoot a problem much faster than looking at the source code. That's especially true for low-level programming.

I'm sure that you'll find other uses when you apply your knowledge about assembly language in the future. It's a handy tool to have in your tool chest, even though you'll probably never work as a full-time assembly language programmer.

Chapter 3.
The 8-bit AVR Architecture

The Arduino Uno and the Arduino Mega 2560 are based on two different 8-bit AVR microcontrollers: the ATmega328P and the ATmega2560. Each of them has a **CPU core**, but also **peripheral features**, like timers/counters and serial interfaces, as well as built-in memories. The combination of these components in one integrated circuit is what makes it a **microcontroller** instead of a CPU. The CPU cores of the ATmega328P and ATmega2560 are very similar, and all the instructions that work on the Uno work on the Mega 2560 too. There are two additional instructions on the Mega 2560, called `eicall` and `eijmp`, and I'll show you later in the book how to handle that in a program that has to work on both the Uno and the Mega 2560.

The 8-bit AVR is a **RISC** (Reduced Instruction Set Computer) architecture. RISC means that the instructions are simple, and many of them execute in one or two clock cycles. To put things in perspective, the Intel processors used in PCs have many complex instructions that execute in tens of clock cycles. Such processors are **CISC** (Complex Instruction Set Computer) architectures.

From an assembly language programming perspective, a PC is a **von Neumann architecture**, which means that data and machine code are in a shared memory address space. The AVR microcontrollers, on the other hand, have data and machine code stored in separate memory address spaces. That's called a **Harvard architecture**. The machine code is stored in a **flash program memory**, while the data is stored in **SRAM** (Static RAM) memory. Even though it's called *Static* RAM, the contents don't survive power cycling. SRAM is faster but also more expensive than ordinary computer memory, called DRAM (Dynamic RAM). There's also **EEPROM** (Electrically Erasable Programmable Read-Only Memory) in the AVR that you can use to store data that must survive power cycling.

In practice, C/C++ variables are often stored in CPU **registers** instead of the SRAM. Each register is an 8-bit memory location inside the CPU core, with a single clock cycle access time in comparison to the two clock cycle access time for the internal SRAM. The AVR architecture has 32 8-bit **general-purpose registers** called r0 to r31. When you want to operate on data, you must copy it to a register first if it's not already there. Instructions such as add (addition), mul (multiplication), and eor (xor), only work on data that is stored in registers. You can think of the registers as a special-purpose fast-access memory, where each byte has its own fixed name. The whole set of 32 registers is called a **register file**. The register file is mapped at the bottom of the **data space** (in contrast to the flash program memory address space). Therefore, data space addresses 0x00 to 0x1f correspond to the registers r0 to r31.

Above the register file in the data space, at the addresses 0x20 to 0x5f, are 64 **I/O registers** that are used for I/O and peripherals. Next follows the **extended I/O registers**. There are more of them in the Mega 2560 than in the Uno, so the Uno address range is 0x60 to 0xff, while the Mega 2560 address range is 0x60 to 0x1ff. Finally, the SRAM memory starts at address 0x100 in the Uno and 0x200 in the Mega 2560.

We're going to use I/O registers many times throughout the book. They are documented in the datasheets of the microcontrollers, together with plenty of other important information about the AVR architecture. You can download the datasheet for the ATmega328P here:

```
http://ww1.microchip.com/downloads/en/DeviceDoc/Atmel-
7810-Automotive-Microcontrollers-ATmega328P_Datasheet.pdf
```

The datasheet for the ATmega2560 is available here:

```
https://ww1.microchip.com/downloads/en/devicedoc/atmel-
2549-8-bit-avr-microcontroller-atmega640-1280-1281-2560-
2561_datasheet.pdf
```

Finally, I want to show you what is called **the order of operands**, or **operand order**, of the AVR architecture. We'll take the `add` instruction as an example:

```
add r2, r3
```

The line above means that the values in `r2` and `r3` are added together, and the result is put in `r2`. The **operands** are what the instruction operates on, in this case, `r2` and `r3`. Here's another example:

```
mov r2, r3
```

This time, the value in `r3` is copied to `r2` (`mov` is short for "move"). We say that `r3` is the **source register**, and `r2` the **destination register**. The destination is on the left when you program in assembly language on the Arduino.

Chapter 4.
Assembly Code in Sketches

Using assembly code in your C/C++ Arduino sketch is both simple and complicated at the same time. It's simple because all you have to do is add an `asm` statement and then you can start putting assembly code in it. It's complicated because you must follow many obscure rules, and you can cause unpredictable bugs that are hard to troubleshoot if you don't. I'm going to explain new rules throughout the book, so don't make the mistake of thinking that this chapter is enough to understand them all.

We'll begin with some code and see how it works, step by step. First, notice that the code has the default `setup()` and `loop()` functions of a typical Arduino sketch:

```
void setup() {
  byte a=1, b=0;

  Serial.begin(9600);
  Serial.print("a=");
  Serial.print(a);
```

```
    Serial.print(" b=");
    Serial.println(b);
    asm volatile (
      "mov r2, %1 \n\t"
      "mov %0, r2 \n\t"
        : "=r"(b)
        : "r"(a)
        : "r2"
    );
    Serial.print("a=");
    Serial.print(a);
    Serial.print(" b=");
    Serial.println(b);
}

void loop() {
}
```

You're probably already familiar with the functions `Serial.begin()`, `Serial.print()`, and `Serial.println()`, but I'll explain how they work just in case.

The line `Serial.begin(9600)` sets the baud rate (the speed) on the connection between the Arduino and your computer. 9600 matches the default setting in the Arduino IDE. The function `Serial.print()` sends text from the Arduino to your computer, without adding a newline at the end. The `Serial.println()` is similar, except it adds a newline.

You use the **serial monitor** in the Arduino IDE to see what the Arduino sends. Click on Tools in the menu bar and then Serial Monitor to open it. Make sure that the baud rate there is still at the default setting 9600.

Understanding the asm Statement

Assembly code in `asm` statements embedded in C/C++ code is called **inline assembly**. Let's look at the `asm` statement in detail:

```
asm volatile (
  "mov r2, %1 \n\t"
```

```
    "mov %0, r2 \n\t"
      : "=r" (b)
      : "r" (a)
      : "r2"
);
```

The word `volatile` is an example of a **qualifier**, and this particular qualifier tells the compiler never to make optimizations that might remove the assembly code. Sometimes, people wrongly assume that the `volatile` qualifier makes the `asm` statement stay in place relative to other `asm` statements. If that's what you need, you must put all the code in the same `asm` statement instead.

Next comes the four different parts of an `asm` statement, separated from each other by colons.

The first part is **the assembler template**, which is where you put the assembly code. You must put each line in double-quotes and end it with the newline-tab-sequence `\n\t`. You can also use a newline without a tab with the Arduino, but it's a common convention to end the lines with newline-tab because some other platforms require it. If you forget to end one or more lines correctly, you'll get the error message "*Error: garbage at end of line.*"

For now, we'll skip the actual assembly code and look at the other parts of the `asm` statement.

The second part is called **the output operands**. It's a comma-separated list of C/C++ variables that the assembly code wants to write to as it runs. You can leave the list empty if you don't need to write to any variables. We use a single output operand in our example:

`"=r" (b)`

The equals sign shows that we're dealing with an output operand, while the `r` means that the compiler is free to pick a suitable general-purpose register to represent the C/C++ variable `b`. Because this is the first variable we add to the list, the register is represented in the assembly code by `%0`. The next one would have been `%1`, and so on. The variable `b` isn't directly visible to the assembly code. Instead, the compiler makes sure that the value in `%0` is copied to b. We don't know beforehand which register the compiler picks, and therefore we must use %0 to represent it.

The third part is called **the input operands**. This list works almost the same way as the output operands list, except that you leave the equals sign out because your assembly code will only read the variables. This is what it looks like in our program:

`"r"(a)`

The compiler makes sure that the C/C++ variable a is copied to a suitable general-purpose register before the assembly code runs. The register is represented by %1 in the assembly code because %0 is already used for our output operand.

I want to show you the output from the program before I explain the fourth part of the asm statement:

```
a=1 b=0
a=1 b=1
```

When the assembly code starts running, %1 holds a copy of the initial value of the a variable. The first mov (**copy register**) instruction copies that value from the register represented by %1 to the r2 register, and the next mov instruction copies it again from r2 to the register represented by %0. The value in %0 is automatically copied to the variable b. All of this results in b changing from 0 to 1, which we can see in the output.

The final part of the asm statement is called **the clobber list**. In our example, it contains a single register:

`"r2"`

The compiler picked the registers to use for %0 and %1, but we picked the register r2 ourselves and copied the content from %1 to it. The compiler is always unaware of what the assembly code in an asm statement means. It only understands C/C++ code. We must warn the compiler if our assembly code changes the value stored in a register, so it doesn't depend on the value staying the same past our code. That's what the clobber list is for—it lists the registers we write to—the registers we **clobber**. If you write to registers without putting them in the clobber list, you will cause unpredictable behavior in the C/C++ code that follows your inline assembly code. You can also cause problems in the inline assembly code itself, because some of the input and output operands may be assigned to the same registers as you use. The ensuing unpredictable behavior can take much time to troubleshoot.

Clobbered Call-Used Registers Must Be in the Clobber List Too

The general-purpose registers r18 to r27, and r30 and r31, are referred to as the **call-used registers**. The compiler lets you use them freely in pure assembly functions, which means that you don't have to save and restore them. It doesn't matter if you don't understand what that means right now. What matters is that you *can not* use them freely in ordinary inline assembly code. If you clobber them, put them in the clobber list!

Never Rely on the Clobber List for r1

The compiler doesn't save and restore the registers you put in the clobber list as it does on some other platforms. Instead, it avoids using the clobber list registers for certain purposes. For example, local variables are only held in registers that aren't in the clobber list. When there are no more registers available, the compiler puts the rest of the local variables in a memory area called the stack. Similarly, the compiler avoids the registers in the clobber list when it picks the ones to use for the input and output operands. If there are no available registers left for input and output operands, you get the following compilation error:

```
error: can't find a register in class 'GENERAL_REGS' while reloading 'asm'
```

This behavior affects the relation between the clobber list and the registers r0 and r1. They're called **the fixed registers** because they're used for fixed purposes. The compiler doesn't use them as ordinary general-purpose registers.

The fixed way `r0` is used allows you to include it in your assembly code without causing any problems. The register `r1`, which is also called **the zero register**, is much more problematic. The surrounding C/C++ code assumes that it always contains the value zero. Putting `r1` in the clobber list *doesn't change* that fact, because the purpose is fixed and using `r1` can't easily be avoided by using another register as the zero register instead. Therefore, you must *always* remember to clear `r1` after you're finished using it in your assembly code. If you forget to clear it, you will cause unpredictable behavior in the C/C++ code that follows.

Let's try our previous sketch again, but this time we change register `r2` to `r1`, and put `r1` in the clobber list:

```
void setup() {
  byte a=1, b=0;

  Serial.begin(9600);
  Serial.print("a=");
  Serial.print(a);
  Serial.print(" b=");
  Serial.println(b);
  asm volatile (
    "mov r1, %1 \n\t"
    "mov %0, r1 \n\t"
    : "=r"(b)
    : "r"(a)
    : "r1"
  );
  Serial.print("a=");
  Serial.print(a);
  Serial.print(" b=");
  Serial.println(b);
}

void loop() {
}
```

Part of the output gets scrambled because of the subtle bug we introduced:

```
a=1 b=0
1? b=1
```

Even though `r1` is in the clobber list, the compiler doesn't save and restore the zero value it contains. When the assembly code finishes, `r1` contains the value 1 instead of 0, and that causes problems in the print routines that are called next.

Sometimes You Can Use Basic asm Statements

The `asm` statements we've used so far are called **extended asm statements**. There's also a more straightforward form, called **basic asm statements**. You can use them when you don't have any variables to input or output and don't need a clobber list. A basic `asm` statement looks like this:

```
asm (
   "nop \n\t"
   "nop \n\t"
   "nop \n\t"
);
```

The assembly code in this example consists of three `nop` (**no operation**) instructions. They do nothing except use up a CPU clock cycle each. This `asm` statement doesn't include a `volatile` qualifier because all basic `asm` statements are implicitly volatile.

Chapter 5.
Hello World: Blinking the Debug LED

Now we'll do something that's probably familiar to you from learning to program the Arduino in C/C++. It's the Arduino equivalent of a Hello World program: blinking the debug LED. I'm going to show you three different ways to do it. Here's the first one:

```
extern "C" {
  __attribute__((used)) void asm_delay(unsigned long d)
  {
    delay(d);
  }
}

void setup() {
}

void loop() {
  asm volatile (
    // Turn debug LED on
```

```
    "ldi  r18,  0b00100000     \n\t"
    "sts  0x24,  r18           \n\t"
    "sts  0x25,  r18           \n\t"

    // Wait 100 ms
    "ldi  r22,  0x64           \n\t"
    "ldi  r23,  0x00           \n\t"
    "ldi  r24,  0x00           \n\t"
    "ldi  r25,  0x00           \n\t"
    "call asm_delay            \n\t"

    // Turn debug LED off
    "ldi  r18,  0b00000000     \n\t"
    "sts  0x25,  r18           \n\t"

    // Wait 1000 ms
    "ldi  r22,  0xe8           \n\t"
    "ldi  r23,  0x03           \n\t"
    "ldi  r24,  0x00           \n\t"
    "ldi  r25,  0x00           \n\t"
    "call asm_delay            \n\t"
    :
    :
    : "r18", "r22", "r23", "r24", "r25"
  );
}
```

Calling the delay() Function from Assembly Code

The first part of the sketch is a C function that helps us call the built-in `delay()` function. If we try to call the `delay()` function straight from the assembly code we'll get the error message *"undefined reference to delay,"* so instead we call our own function `asm_delay()`. It passes the delay in milliseconds to the built-in `delay()` function. We declare it `extern "C"` to prevent the compiler from mangling the function name. To make sure that the compiler generates the code for the function even though it isn't referenced anywhere we also use `__attribute__((used))`. The compiler doesn't understand the assembly code, and therefore it can't see that we call the `asm_delay()` function. Without the `used` attribute, the compiler could remove the function, which would lead to the error message *"undefined reference to asm_delay."* You might find that removing `extern "C"` and `__attribute__((used))` doesn't break anything, or that the sketch works fine without one but not without the other. Nevertheless, the sketch won't work with some other versions of the Arduino IDE unless you keep both of them.

While we're at it, we might as well look at the code that calls the `asm_delay()` function. It's used twice, with a small difference, and I'll repeat the second version here:

```
"ldi r22, 0xe8          \n\t"
"ldi r23, 0x03          \n\t"
"ldi r24, 0x00          \n\t"
"ldi r25, 0x00          \n\t"
"call asm_delay         \n\t"
```

The `ldi` instruction is called **load immediate**, and it loads an 8-bit constant into a register. If we put the four constants together to form 0x000003e8, and then convert that number to decimal, we get 1000. This is how the unsigned long parameter 1000 milliseconds is passed to the `delay()` function. The arguments to a function are passed, from left to right, through the registers `r25`, `r24`, and downward to `r8`. If more space is needed, the remaining arguments are pushed onto a memory area called the stack, which I will cover in a later chapter. Finally, the `call` instruction calls the function `asm_delay()`. The whole assembly code block does the same thing as the following line of C/C++ code:

```
asm_delay(1000);
```

Blinking the Debug LED Through the Data Space

It's time to turn on and off the debug LED. In C/C++ you would first set pin 13 as an output, and then turn the LED on, like so:

```
pinMode(13, OUTPUT);
digitalWrite(13, HIGH);
```

We do almost the same thing in assembly code, but there's no such concept as pin 13 at that level. Instead, we have two **ports** called D and B. Port D is connected to pins 0 to 7, while port B is connected to pins 8 to 13. Bit 0 of port B corresponds to pin 8, bit 1 to pin 9, and so on until we get to bit 5 for pin 13.

To set pin 13 to HIGH, we must set bit 5 of the two I/O registers that control port B. The first one is called DDRB, which stands for Data Direction Register B. Each bit there determines whether the corresponding pin is used as an input or output. We set bit 5 to 1, which means that pin 13 is used as an output. Finally, we must set the corresponding bit in the PORTB register, which sets pin 13 to HIGH, and turns on the debug LED. DDRB is located at data space address 0x24 and PORTB at 0x25.

We begin by setting bit 5 in the `r18` register to 1:

```
"ldi r18, 0b00100000   \n\t"
```

Next, we use the `sts` (**store direct to data space**) instruction to write the value in `r18` to the addresses 0x24 and 0x25 in the data space:

```
"sts 0x24, r18         \n\t"
"sts 0x25, r18         \n\t"
```

To turn the debug LED off, we set bit 5 in the PORTB register to 0:

```
"ldi r18, 0b00000000   \n\t"
"sts 0x25, r18         \n\t"
```

Notice how we clear all the other bits in the DDRB and PORTB registers at the same time as we set and clear bit 5. It's not ideal, but it works for our purposes, and I'll show you a better way later.

Blinking the Debug LED Through the I/O Space

Using the `sts` instruction to control pin 13 through the data space works, but there's a more efficient way. Each execution of `sts` takes two clock cycles, and the instruction is four bytes long. We can do the same thing in one clock cycle and two bytes using the `out` (**store register to I/O location**) instruction.

There is, however, one crucial difference to be aware of. While the `sts` instruction writes to the data space, the `out` instruction writes to the **I/O space**. The I/O registers that are mapped into the data space between the addresses 0x20 and 0x5f are also reachable through the I/O space addresses 0x00 to 0x3f. Add 0x20 to any I/O space address to get the corresponding data space address, or subtract 0x20 from any data space address to get the I/O space address. In our example, we subtract 0x20 from 0x24 and 0x25 to get 0x04 and 0x05 to reach **DDRB** and **PORTB**.

Now we have everything we need to make a new sketch with the `out` instruction instead:

```
extern "C" {
  __attribute__((used)) void asm_delay(unsigned long d)
  {
    delay(d);
  }
}

void setup() {
}

void loop() {
  asm volatile (
  // Turn debug LED on
    "ldi r18, 0b00100000    \n\t"
    "out 0x04, r18          \n\t"
    "out 0x05, r18          \n\t"

  // Wait 100 ms
    "ldi r22, 0x64          \n\t"
    "ldi r23, 0x00          \n\t"
    "ldi r24, 0x00          \n\t"
    "ldi r25, 0x00          \n\t"
    "call asm_delay         \n\t"

  // Turn debug LED off
    "ldi r18, 0b00000000    \n\t"
    "out 0x05, r18          \n\t"
```

```
    // Wait 1000 ms
      "ldi  r22, 0xe8          \n\t"
      "ldi  r23, 0x03          \n\t"
      "ldi  r24, 0x00          \n\t"
      "ldi  r25, 0x00          \n\t"
      "call asm_delay          \n\t"
      :
      :
      : "r18", "r22", "r23", "r24", "r25"
    );
}
```

Blinking the Debug LED With More Precision

Our first two sketches for blinking the debug LED had a shortcoming. We changed the settings for all of the pins controlled by port B because we wrote to the whole registers at once. The best solution is to use the instructions `sbi` (**set bit in I/O register**) and `cbi` (**clear bit in I/O register**). They set and clear a single bit at a time. To set bit 5 in the DDRB register, we use:

```
"sbi 0x04, 5 \n\t"
```

Both instructions work with the I/O space, just like the `out` instruction. However, they can only reach the addresses 0x00 to 0x1f, while the `out` instruction can reach the broader range 0x00 to 0x3f. Here's the new sketch for blinking the debug LED with more precision:

```
extern "C" {
  __attribute__((used)) void asm_delay(unsigned long d)
  {
    delay(d);
  }
}

void setup() {
}

void loop() {
  asm volatile (
    // Turn debug LED on
```

```
        "sbi 0x04, 5              \n\t"
        "sbi 0x05, 5              \n\t"

        // Wait 100 ms
        "ldi r22, 0x64            \n\t"
        "ldi r23, 0x00            \n\t"
        "ldi r24, 0x00            \n\t"
        "ldi r25, 0x00            \n\t"
        "call asm_delay           \n\t"

        // Turn debug LED off
        "cbi 0x05, 5              \n\t"

        // Wait 1000 ms
        "ldi r22, 0xe8            \n\t"
        "ldi r23, 0x03            \n\t"
        "ldi r24, 0x00            \n\t"
        "ldi r25, 0x00            \n\t"
        "call asm_delay           \n\t"
        :
        :
        : "r22", "r23", "r24", "r25"
    );
}
```

Chapter 6.
Constraints

You've already seen constraints in action without knowing it. Here's an `asm` statement we've used before:

```
asm volatile (
  "mov r2, %1 \n\t"
  "mov %0, r2 \n\t"
    : "=r"(b)
    : "r"(a)
    : "r2"
);
```

A **constraint** limits where the compiler may store an input or output operand for the assembly code. The letter `r` in the example above tells the compiler that it must put `%0` and `%1` in two of the registers `r2` to `r31`. The symbol = is a **constraint modifier**. This particular modifier means that the variable may only be used for output.

The `r` constraint is an example of a **simple constraint**, which is generic and can be used on other architectures too. It refers to a general-purpose register, but the general-purpose registers `r0` and `r1` are never assigned by the compiler for the `r` constraint because they are fixed registers. If you somehow manage to use all the other available registers, the compiler stops with the following error message:

```
error: can't find a register in class 'GENERAL_REGS' while reloading 'asm'
```

How to Choose Constraints

The compiler supports several different constraints, and you should choose constraints that match the instructions you use. Some instructions only work with some of the registers, or with some types of constants. For example, the `ldi` instruction only works with the registers `r16` to `r31`. Those registers are called **the upper registers**, and the corresponding constraint is d. Another example is the `mulsu` instruction which multiplies signed numbers with unsigned numbers. It only works with the registers `r16` to `r23`, which are called **the simple upper registers**, and the corresponding constraint is a. I'll introduce more constraints one at a time when we need them.

Using Constants Instead of Magic Numbers

We've used several magic numbers in our code. For example, I/O port numbers and bit numbers like these:

```
"sbi 0x04, 5          \n\t"
"sbi 0x05, 5          \n\t"
```

Another solution is to use pre-defined C/C++ constants that we pass as input operands. Here's a new version of the LED blinking sketch—this time with constants:

```
extern "C" {
  __attribute__((used)) void asm_delay(unsigned long d)
  {
    delay(d);
  }
}

void setup() {
```

```
}

void loop() {
  asm volatile (
    // Turn debug LED on
    "sbi %0, %2        \n\t"
    "sbi %1, %3        \n\t"

    // Wait 100 ms
    "ldi r22, 0x64     \n\t"
    "ldi r23, 0x00     \n\t"
    "ldi r24, 0x00     \n\t"
    "ldi r25, 0x00     \n\t"
    "call asm_delay    \n\t"

    // Turn debug LED off
    "cbi %1, %3        \n\t"

    // Wait 1000 ms
    "ldi r22, 0xe8     \n\t"
    "ldi r23, 0x03     \n\t"
    "ldi r24, 0x00     \n\t"
    "ldi r25, 0x00     \n\t"
    "call asm_delay    \n\t"
    :
    : "I" (_SFR_IO_ADDR(DDRB)), "I"
      (_SFR_IO_ADDR(PORTB)), "I" (DDB5), "I" (PB5)
    : "r22", "r23", "r24", "r25"
  );
}
```

There are four new input operands in this version, each with the constraint I, which means a 6-bit positive integer constant. The first constant is DDRB, wrapped in the _SFR_IO_ADDR() macro. **SFR** stands for **Special Function Registers**, and it refers to the I/O space registers. The DDRB constant is 0x24, and the _SFR_IO_ADDR() macro subtracts 0x20 from it, so we get the I/O space address 0x04 for the DDRB register. The PORTB constant, 0x25, is wrapped in the same way to get the address 0x05. Finally, we have two other constants: DDB5 and PB5. Both are equal to 5 and are used to set bit 5 of the DDRB and PORTB registers. You can also use the constant PORTB5 instead of PB5—they are both equal to 5.

Passing Input Operands Longer Than One Byte

We still had some magic numbers in the last version of the LED blink sketch. They were used to determine how many milliseconds to keep the LED on and off. Here's a new version where we store those numbers in two variables called on_delay and off_delay:

```
unsigned long on_delay = 100;
unsigned long off_delay = 1000;

extern "C" {
  __attribute__((used)) void asm_delay(unsigned long d)
  {
    delay(d);
  }
}

void setup() {
}

void loop() {
  asm volatile (
    // Turn debug LED on
    "sbi %0, %2        \n\t"
    "sbi %1, %3        \n\t"

    // Wait 100 ms
    "mov r22, %A4      \n\t"
    "mov r23, %B4      \n\t"
    "mov r24, %C4      \n\t"
    "mov r25, %D4      \n\t"
    "call asm_delay    \n\t"

    // Turn debug LED off
    "cbi %1, %3        \n\t"

    // Wait 1000 ms
```

```
        "mov r22, %A5      \n\t"
        "mov r23, %B5      \n\t"
        "mov r24, %C5      \n\t"
        "mov r25, %D5      \n\t"
        "call asm_delay    \n\t"
        :
        : "I" (_SFR_IO_ADDR(DDRB)), "I"
          (_SFR_IO_ADDR(PORTB)), "I" (DDB5), "I" (PB5), "r"
          (on_delay), "r" (off_delay)
        : "r22", "r23", "r24", "r25"
    );
}
```

We pass `on_delay` and `off_delay` as two input operands with the `r` constraint, but this time they are 32-bit numbers instead of 8-bit numbers. That's a potential problem because the registers are only 8 bits wide. We must have our two 32-bit numbers split into four 8-bit ones each. That's easy to do by adding upper-case letters to `%4` and `%5`. The least significant byte of the `%4` operand is represented by `%A4` and the most significant byte by `%D4`. If these were 16-bit numbers, we would only use `A` and `B`, but since they are 32-bit numbers, we use `A`, `B`, `C`, and `D`.

Chapter 7.
A Closer Look at How Instructions Work

Let's focus on a single instruction and understand it in detail. Here's a new sketch:

```
void setup() {
  byte sum;

  Serial.begin(9600);
  asm volatile (
   "ldi r16, 15    \n\t"
   "ldi r17, 37    \n\t"
   "add r16, r17   \n\t"
   "mov %0, r16    \n\t"
    : "=r"(sum)
    :
    : "r16", "r17"
  );
  Serial.print("sum=");
  Serial.println(sum);
}

void loop() {
```

}

The assembly code puts 15 in `r16` and 37 in `r17`. Now we're ready for the instruction that I'm going to build this chapter around: `add`.

Understanding the AVR Assembly Documentation

You can find the AVR assembly instruction set manual in PDF form here:

`http://ww1.microchip.com/downloads/en/devicedoc/atmel-0856-avr-instruction-set-manual.pdf`

There's also a convenient web-based version:

`https://www.microchip.com/webdoc/avrassembler/`

The documentation for `add` starts like this:

> **Description:**
>
> Adds two registers without the C flag and places the result in the destination register Rd.
>
> Operation:
>
> Rd ← Rd + Rr
>
> Syntax: Operands: Program Counter:
>
> ADD Rd,Rr $0 \leq d \leq 31$, $0 \leq r \leq 31$, PC ← PC + 1

`Rd` and `Rr` are part of **the instruction set nomenclature**, which is a systematic way of naming things related to the instruction set. Rd is used to represent a register that is both a **destination** and a **source**, while Rr represents a source register. The `add` instruction adds the values in two registers, `Rd` and `Rr`, and stores the result in `Rd`. That's why `Rd` is both a source and a destination at the same time. The whole process is also described using this notation:

```
Rd ← Rd + Rr
```

Next comes the actual syntax:

```
ADD Rd, Rr
```

Compare that to our sketch, and you'll notice that the documentation calls the instruction ADD, while I've called it `add`. Inline assembly code is traditionally written in lowercase, but the sketch still works if you change `add` to `ADD`.

The documentation also states that you can use any two registers from `r0` to `r31`, and it does so with the following mathematical expressions, where d and r represent the register numbers:

$0 \leq d \leq 31$

$0 \leq r \leq 31$

Finally, we have this cryptic thing to decode:

```
PC ← PC + 1
```

PC stands for **Program Counter**, which is a register that can't be read directly by assembly code. It contains the address of the *next* instruction to execute, counted in 16-bit words—*not* in bytes. The reason is that nearly all instructions have 16-bit opcodes. The exceptions are `jmp` and `call`, which have 32-bit opcodes. The PC is incremented by one each time the `add` instruction executes, because the opcode is 16-bit, and the Program Counter counts in 16-bit words.

What It Looks Like in Machine Code

The `add` instruction encoded in 16 bits looks like this:

```
0000 11rd dddd rrrr
```

In our example, `Rd` is `r16`, and `Rr` is `r17`. 16 in binary is 10000, and 17 is 10001. The most significant bits are 1 in both cases, so we can write the `0000 11rd` part as `0000 1111` since the `r` and `d` correspond to the most significant bits of the register numbers. Next, we can write the `dddd rrrr` part as `0000 0001`, where `0000` and `0001` correspond to the four least significant bits of the register numbers. Thus, the machine code for `add r16, r17` is:

```
0000 1111 0000 0001
```

If we convert that to hexadecimal, we get:

```
0f 01
```

For comparison, I've disassembled the machine code generated from our sketch, and there the instruction looks like this:

```
01 0f       add r16, r17
```

The AVR microcontrollers are **little-endian**, which means that the least significant byte comes first, at the lower address. When we encoded the instruction and got the result 0f 01, the least significant byte was 01. The disassembly, on the other hand, presents the machine code with the byte at the lower memory address first. Both versions are the same—just presented in two different ways.

The Status Register

The **status register**, or **SREG**, is a special kind of register that contains information about the state of the microcontroller. The bits in the status register are called **flags**. Here's what the SREG looks like:

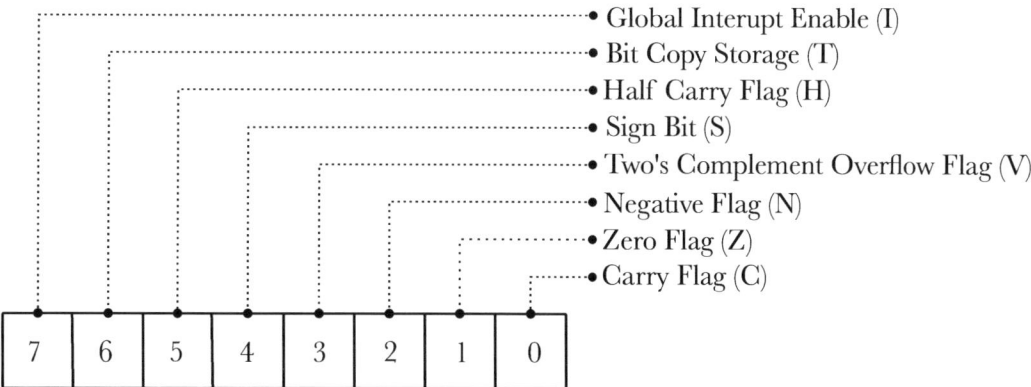

The flags aren't related to each other except for the fact that they are in the SREG and show some kind of state, so explaining all of them at the same time doesn't make sense. I'll introduce the meaning of some of them in the appropriate contexts throughout the book.

To reach the SREG, you can use a constant called __SREG__ in inline assembly code. Here's a sketch that prints the value of __SREG__:

```
void setup() {
  byte sreg_value;

  Serial.begin(9600);
  asm volatile (
    "ldi %0, __SREG__ \n\t"
    : "=r"(sreg_value)
    :
    :
  );
  Serial.print("__SREG__=");
  Serial.println(sreg_value, HEX);
}

void loop() {
}
```

The output is:

__SREG__=3F

This *isn't* the value in the SREG register, but instead the I/O space address where it's located. Notice how the following sketch doesn't compile:

```
void setup() {
  Serial.begin(9600);
  Serial.print("__SREG__=");
  Serial.println(__SREG__, HEX);
}

void loop() {
}
```

Instead, we get the error message:

```
error: '__SREG__' was not declared in this scope
```

That's because __SREG__ can only be used in assembly code—not in C/C++ code.

An SREG Flag Example: The Carry Flag

Here's a sketch that demonstrates add and the Carry Flag:

```
void setup() {
  byte sreg_value_carry, result_carry,
       sreg_value_no_carry, result_no_carry;

  Serial.begin(9600);
  asm volatile (

     // Addition that sets the Carry Flag
     "ldi   r16, 97          \n\t"
     "ldi   r17, 162         \n\t"
     "add   r16, r17         \n\t"
     "mov   %0, r16          \n\t"
     "in    r16, __SREG__    \n\t"
     "mov   %1, r16          \n\t"
```

```
    // Addition that doesn't set the Carry Flag
    "ldi   r16, 9              \n\t"
    "ldi   r17, 16             \n\t"
    "add   r16, r17            \n\t"
    "mov   %2, r16             \n\t"
    "in    r16, __SREG__       \n\t"
    "mov %3, r16               \n\t"

    : "=r" (result_carry), "=r" (sreg_value_carry), "=r"
      (result_no_carry), "=r" (sreg_value_no_carry)
    :
    : "r16", "r17"
  );
  Serial.print("Result with Carry Flag set=");
  Serial.println(result_carry);
  Serial.print("SREG with Carry Flag set=");
  Serial.println(sreg_value_carry, HEX);
  Serial.print("Result without Carry Flag set=");
  Serial.println(result_no_carry);
  Serial.print("SREG without Carry Flag set=");
  Serial.println(sreg_value_no_carry, HEX);
}

void loop() {
}
```

First, we add the numbers 97 and 162. The result is 259, but there's a problem: it takes more than one byte to store 259. In binary, the result is 0000 0001 0000 0011. Only the least significant bit of the upper byte is set, and we say that the addition has resulted in a **carry**. The result of the addition is 3 because that's the content of the lower byte, and the Carry Flag is set to 1. We can also say that the Carry Flag is **set**, which means that it's set to 1. If the Carry Flag were set to 0 instead, we would say that it's **cleared**.

Next, we add the two numbers 9 and 16. This time everything is straightforward because the result is 25, which fits in one byte. The Carry Flag is cleared this time because the addition doesn't result in a carry.

Here's what the sketch prints:

```
Result with Carry Flag set=3
SREG with Carry Flag set=129
Result without Carry Flag set=25
SREG without Carry Flag set=128
```

The Carry Flag is bit 0 in the SREG. If we convert 129 and 128 to binary, we get 1000 0001 and 1000 0000. As you can see, the least significant bit is 1 when we get a carry, and 0 when we don't get a carry.

Chapter 8.
The Pointer Register Pairs

The three 16-bit **pointer register pairs** overlap with the six highest general-purpose registers. The pointer register x is r27:r26, which means that the most significant byte is in r27 and the least significant byte is in r26. The y register is r29:r28, and the z register is r31:r30.

Using a Pointer Register Pair

This sketch uses the x register to print the characters A V R:

```
const char *s = "AVR";

void setup() {
  byte pl, ph;
  char ch1, ch2, ch3;

  pl = ((unsigned short) s) & 0xff;
  ph = ((unsigned short) s) >> 8;
  asm volatile (
    "mov   r26, %3    \n\t"
    "mov   xh,  %4    \n\t"
```

```
    "ld    %0,    x+      \n\t"
    "ld    %1,    x+      \n\t"
    "ld    %2,    x       \n\t"
    : "=r" (ch1), "=r" (ch2), "=r" (ch3)
    : "r" (pl), "r" (ph)
    : "r26", "r27"
  );
  Serial.begin(9600);
  Serial.println(ch1);
  Serial.println(ch2);
  Serial.println(ch3);
}

void loop() {
}
```

The variable s points to the string "AVR" in the SRAM. The following lines of code put the low byte of the address in pl and the high byte in ph:

```
pl = ((unsigned short) s) & 0xff;
ph = ((unsigned short) s) >> 8;
```

The assembly code copies the values from pl (%3) and ph (%4) into r26 and xh. The register xh is the high byte of x, which is the same as r27. I've chosen to mix r26 and xh to illustrate both variants, but you should always stick to either r26 and r27, or xl and xh.

Next comes a sequence of assembly instructions that put the characters from the string into the output operands ch1 (%0), ch2 (%1), and ch3 (%3):

```
"ld    %0,    x+      \n\t"
"ld    %1,    x+      \n\t"
"ld    %2,    x       \n\t"
```

There are two essential things to understand here. The first is what the ld instruction does. The AVR documentation describes ld like this: **load indirect** from data space to register using index x. ld doesn't copy the content of x. Instead, it uses the address that is stored in x to copy the byte that x *points to*. The second thing to understand is the difference between x+ and x. When we write x+, x is incremented by one before the *next* instruction executes. We say that x is **post incremented**. That's how the three assembly instructions can copy all the three letters in the string and not just the first one. The final instruction doesn't need to increment x because we're done copying by then.

There's also a **pre-decrement** version. It looks like this:

"ld   %1, -x   \n\t"

If we write -x, x is decremented by one before the ld instruction executes.

Pointer Register Pairs and Constraints

There are a few constraints that limit the input and output operands to pointer register pairs. They're presented in the following table:

Constraint	Pointer Register Pairs
b	x, y
e	x, y, z
x	x
y	y
z	z

Chapter 9.
Basic Jumping and Branching

Jumping in assembly code works like `goto` in C/C++, except it doesn't have a bad reputation like `goto`. Here's an example of jumping, with the instruction `jmp`:

```
void setup() {
  byte result = 0;

  asm volatile (
    "ldi   r16, 10    \n\t"
    "jmp   1f         \n\t"
    "ldi   r16, 20    \n\t"
    "1: mov %0, r16   \n\t"
    : "=r" (result)
    :
    : "r16"
  );
  Serial.begin(9600);
  Serial.println(result);
```

```
}

void loop() {
}
```

After loading the value 10 into `r16`, the execution doesn't continue at the next line, but at label 1 because of the `jmp`. That's why the sketch prints 10—not 20—to the serial monitor.

The jump destination is written as `1f` instead of just `1`. The reason is that the same label can be used more than once in the same `asm` statement, and `f` (forward) specifies that the target is the *next* label 1. If we also had a label 1 *before* the jump, we would go there with the target `1b` (backward). Even if you *can* use the same label more than once, it increases the risk that you mix up the labels and thereby introduce bugs.

The label we used is a number, but we could have used a name instead, like this:

```
jmp my_label
...
my_label:
```

As good as it looks, there's an excellent reason not to do so. Sometimes the compiler generates duplicates of inline assembly code for optimization purposes. When that happens, there will be multiple copies of the same label. That leads to a compilation error, because the symbol is already defined. In contrast, a label that consists of a number and a colon is always transformed into a symbol that is guaranteed to be unique.

Relative Jumps

We have already used the `jmp` instruction, but there's also an instruction called `rjmp` (**relative jump**). The difference is that while `jmp` can target any address in the program memory, `rjmp` can only target 4 KB before and after the instruction itself. We save some space and clock cycles in return. The `jmp` instruction is encoded using 4 bytes and needs 3 clock cycles, while the `rjmp` instruction is encoded using 2 bytes and only needs 2 clock cycles.

Branching Instructions

The **branching instructions** are **conditional** jumps—they only perform the jump under certain conditions. In all other cases, the execution continues with the instruction on the line below. The AVR microcontroller has several different branching instructions, all of which depend on the flags in the SREG. We'll look at one of the branching instructions in more detail because if you understand one of them, you can use the AVR documentation to figure out how to use the rest. Besides, there's another chapter toward the end of the book that covers more branching and jumping.

This time we'll compare two sketches with one small difference between them. In the first version, we store 10 in `r16` and 11 in `r17`, while in the second version we do it the other way around. Here's the first version:

```
void setup() {
  byte result;

  asm volatile (
    "ldi    r16, 10     \n\t"
    "ldi    r17, 11     \n\t"
    "cp     r16, r17    \n\t"
    "brlo 1f            \n\t"
    "ldi    %0, 17      \n\t"
    "jmp    2f          \n\t"
    "1: ldi %0, 16      \n\t"
    "2:                 \n\t"
    : "=d" (result)
    :
    : "r16", "r17"
  );
  Serial.begin(9600);
  Serial.print("The register with the lower value was r");
  Serial.println(result);
}

void loop() {
```

}

There are two new instructions in the sketch: cp (**compare**) and brlo (**branch if lower**). The cp instruction compares the values in r16 and r17 by calculating r16-r17. The result of the subtraction is thrown away, but the relevant flags in the SREG are updated. The SREG flags are then used by the brlo instruction to determine if the value in r16 is lower than that in r17 or not. We continue at label 1 if r16 holds the lower value, and there we load 16 into the output operand result (%0). If r16 doesn't hold the lower value, the execution continues with the next instruction after brlo, which loads 17 into result (%0).

Since 10 in r16 is lower than 11 in r17, the output is:

```
The register with the lower value was r16
```

Here's the second version:

```
void setup() {
  byte result;

  asm volatile (
    "ldi    r16, 11   \n\t"
    "ldi    r17, 10   \n\t"
    "cp     r16, r17  \n\t"
    "brlo 1f          \n\t"
    "ldi    %0, 17    \n\t"
    "jmp    2f        \n\t"
    "1: ldi %0, 16    \n\t"
    "2:               \n\t"
    : "=d" (result)
    :
    : "r16", "r17"
  );
  Serial.begin(9600);
  Serial.print("The register with the lower value was r");
  Serial.println(result);
}
```

```
void loop() {
}
```

The output this time is the opposite:

```
The register with the lower value was r17
```

The Importance of Picking the Correct Constraint

There's one small detail that's different in the two sketches above compared to our earlier sketches. Did you spot it? The constraint for the output operand wasn't `r` this time, but `d`. That's because we used `ldi` to load constants into the output operand, and `ldi` is limited to working with `r16` to `r31`. In all the other sketches we've used `mov` or `ld`, and those instructions can work with any register from `r0` to `r31`.

The constraint `d` limits the compiler to picking a register between `r16` and `r31`. If you change the constraint from `d` to `r`, you'll notice that the sketch sometimes compiles fine regardless. Then, if you change something else in the code, it suddenly doesn't compile anymore. That's because the compiler picks different registers depending on what other code you put around the `asm` statement. Sometimes it picks a register between `r16` and `r31` by plain luck, and you won't notice that you've chosen the wrong constraint. Other times it picks a register below `r16`, and then the sketch won't compile.

Chapter 10.
The Stack

The **stack** is an area in the SRAM. You **push** data onto the stack and **pop** it off, in a **LIFO** (**Last In First Out**) fashion.

Here's a stack that starts with one item and then another item is pushed onto it:

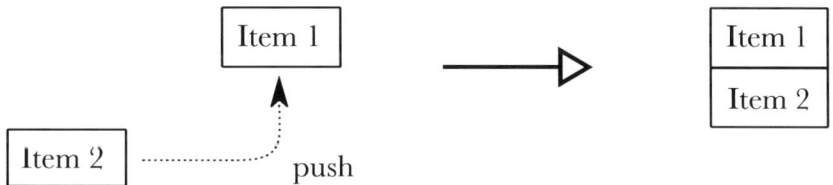

Notice how the stack grows downward. Next, a third item is pushed onto it:

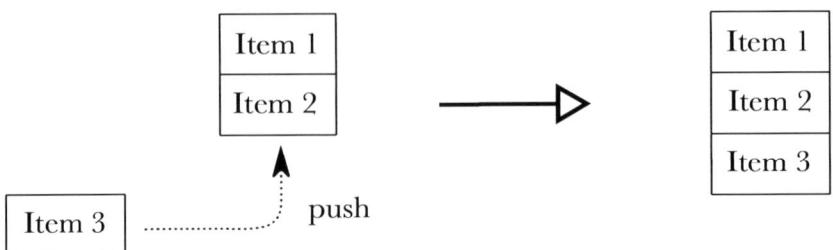

If we wish to remove item 2 we must pop item 3 off the stack first as it works in a LIFO fashion:

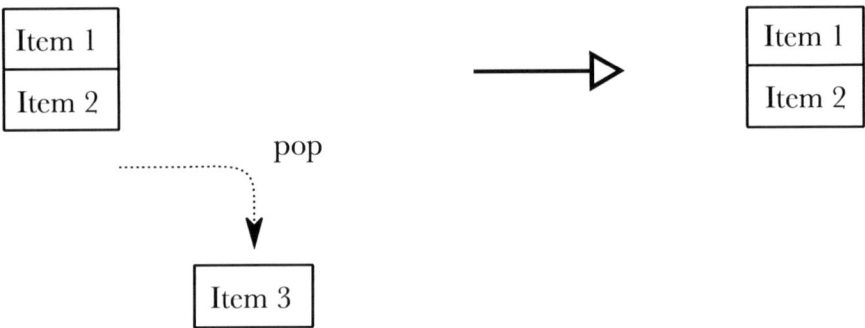

Now we can also pop item 2 off the stack:

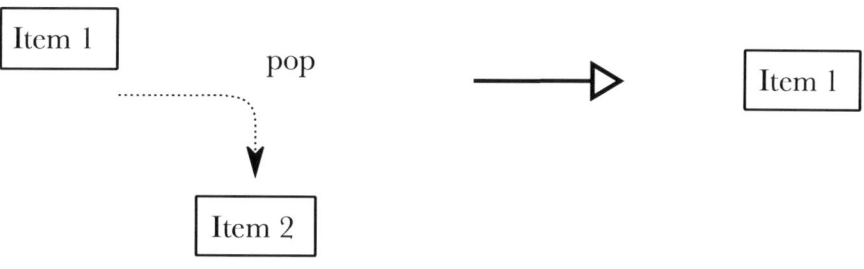

Finally, we can push item 3 back onto the stack, and the end result is that we've removed item 2:

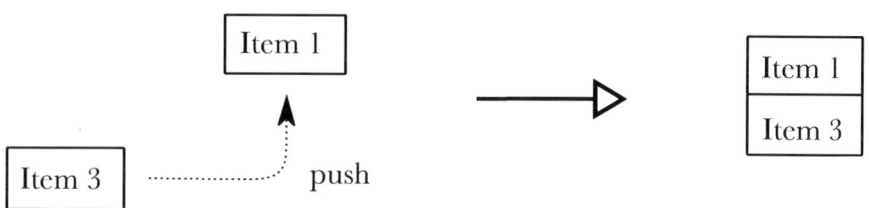

The Stack Pointer

The next free address of the stack is pointed to by the **stack pointer**, which consists of a high (**SPH**) and a low (**SPL**) address byte. You can reach the stack pointer bytes through the data space addresses 0x5d and 0x5e, or the I/O space addresses 0x3d and 0x3e.

Here's a sketch that prints the stack pointer value:

```
void setup() {
  byte spl, sph;
```

```
    asm volatile (
      "in   %0, 0x3d   \n\t"
      "in   %1, 0x3e   \n\t"
      : "=r" (spl), "=r" (sph)
      :
      :
    );
    Serial.begin(9600);
    Serial.print("SP: ");
    Serial.print(sph, HEX);
    Serial.println(spl, HEX);
    Serial.print("RAMEND: ");
    Serial.println(RAMEND, HEX);
}

void loop() {
}
```

Notice how SPL is printed straight after SPH without any whitespace between them. That way, the whole 16-bit stack pointer is printed as one item. The sketch also prints something called RAMEND, which I'll explain shortly.

On my Arduino Uno, with 2048 bytes of SRAM, the sketch outputs the following:

```
SP: 8FD
RAMEND: 8FF
```

On my Arduino Mega 2560, with 8192 bytes of SRAM, the output is:

```
SP: 21FC
RAMEND: 21FF
```

The Arduino Uno has a total of 0x100 register bytes below the SRAM in the data space, while the Arduino Mega 2560 has a total of 0x200 register bytes. These numbers come from the Register Summary section of the ATmega328P and ATmega2560 datasheets. 2048 (0x800) bytes plus 0x100 bytes equals 0x900 bytes, while 8192 (0x2000) bytes plus 0x200 bytes equals 0x2200 bytes.

Since the data space starts at address zero, the highest SRAM address in the Arduino Uno is 0x900 minus one, which equals 0x8ff. In the Arduino Mega 2560, the highest SRAM address is 0x2000 minus one, which equals 0x21ff. Now it's obvious what RAMEND means—it's the highest SRAM address.

As you can see, the stack pointer is located close to the highest SRAM address in both cases. That's because the stack starts at RAMEND and grows downward. The stack pointer is automatically initialized to RAMEND when the microcontroller is powered up.

Push and Pop

The instructions push and pop are used to store data on the stack and then retrieve it, as demonstrated by this sketch:

```
void setup() {
  byte result = 0;

  asm volatile (
    "ldi   r16, 10    \n\t"
    "push  r16        \n\t"
    "ldi   r16, 20    \n\t"
    "pop   r16        \n\t"
    "mov   %0, r16    \n\t"
    : "=r" (result)
    :
    : "r16"
  );
  Serial.begin(9600);
  Serial.print("r16=");
  Serial.println(result);
}

void loop() {
}
```

The sketch loads 10 into r16 and then pushes it onto the stack. Next, it overwrites the content of r16 with the value 20. The original value would have been lost if we hadn't saved it on the stack, but now we can pop it off and back into r16. The output shows that r16 still contains 10 even though it was briefly overwritten:

r16=10

Function Arguments and the Stack

Function calls use the stack for two different purposes: to store the return address of the function call, and to store any function arguments that don't fit into the general-purpose registers.

Let's investigate how the stack is used to pass function arguments that don't fit in the general-purpose registers. Here's a new C/C++ sketch:

```
void __attribute__((noinline)) f(byte b1, byte b2, byte
    b3, byte b4, byte b5, byte b6, byte b7, byte b8,
byte b9, byte b10, byte b11, byte b12)
{
  Serial.println(b1);
  Serial.println(b2);
  Serial.println(b3);
  Serial.println(b4);
  Serial.println(b5);
  Serial.println(b6);
  Serial.println(b7);
  Serial.println(b8);
  Serial.println(b9);
  Serial.println(b10);
  Serial.println(b11);
  Serial.println(b12);
}

void setup() {
  byte b1 = random();
  byte b2 = random();
  byte b3 = random();
  byte b4 = random();
  byte b5 = random();
  byte b6 = random();
```

```
  byte b7 = random();
  byte b8 = random();
  byte b9 = random();
  byte b10 = random();
  byte b11 = random();
  byte b12 = random();

  Serial.begin(9600);
  f(b1, b2, b3, b4, b5, b6, b7, b8, b9, b10, b11, b12);
}

void loop() {
}
```

We must make sure that the compiler generates a function instead of merely inlining the code inside the `setup()` function. We do that by putting `__attribute__((noinline))` in the function definition. The next problem is that if we pass constants as arguments to the function, the compiler will simply include them in it to optimize the code instead of passing them to it. We have to trick the compiler somehow, and we do so by passing random numbers to the function. Since those numbers aren't known at compile time, the compiler can't optimize the function arguments away.

Now, let's look at the relevant parts of the disassembly:

```
call     0x7a2    ; 0x7a2 <random>
mov      r28, r22
call     0x7a2    ; 0x7a2 <random>
mov      r29, r22
call     0x7a2    ; 0x7a2 <random>
mov      r17, r22
call     0x7a2    ; 0x7a2 <random>
mov      r15, r22
call     0x7a2    ; 0x7a2 <random>
mov      r16, r22
call     0x7a2    ; 0x7a2 <random>
mov      r14, r22
call     0x7a2    ; 0x7a2 <random>
mov      r12, r22
call     0x7a2    ; 0x7a2 <random>
```

```
mov     r10, r22
call    0x7a2    ; 0x7a2 <random>
mov     r8, r22
call    0x7a2    ; 0x7a2 <random>
mov     r13, r22
call    0x7a2    ; 0x7a2 <random>
mov     r11, r22
call    0x7a2    ; 0x7a2 <random>
.
.
.
push    r22
push    r11
push    r13
mov     r18, r15
mov     r20, r17
mov     r22, r29
mov     r24, r28
call    0x38c
```

The random() function returns a long, which is a 32-bit value on the Arduino, and the convention is to return such values in r22 to r25. Since we assign the random numbers to byte-sized variables, we only need the least significant byte, which is in r22. That's why a mov from r22 to another register follows each call to random().

Perhaps you've noticed that the compiler has taken a bit of detour when generating the code. Instead of putting three of the random numbers straight into r18, r20, and r24, it first put them into r15, r17, and r28, and then copied them to the correct registers later. The reason is that the registers r18-r27 (as well as r30-r31) can be used freely by the target of a function call without saving and restoring them. The random() function trashes the content in r18, r20, and r24 each time we call it. Don't worry about this phenomenon for now, because I'll cover it in much more detail in the next chapter.

When the call to f() is made (call 0x38c), the registers r24, r22, r20, r18, r16, r14, r12, r10, and r8 contain the first nine arguments. As you can see in the C/C++ code, there are twelve arguments in total, and the last three are pushed onto the stack instead of passed in registers. The **function calling convention** of AVR assembly is to pass arguments from left to right in the registers `r25` to `r8`. All arguments are aligned to start in even-numbered registers for optimization purposes, which means that our byte-sized arguments have an unused register above them. That's why the first argument is put in `r24` instead of `r25`, and the next one follows in `r22` instead of `r23`, and so on. The first nine arguments are enough to fill all the available registers that are used for argument passing, and that's why the compiler passes the other three on the stack.

Function Return Addresses and the Stack

When a function is called with the `call` instruction, the **return address** is pushed onto the stack. It's the address of the instruction that follows directly after `call`. When the function returns, the `ret` instruction pops the return address off the stack and uses it to determine where to continue the execution. In the following sketch, the return address is the address of `jmp 2f`:

```
void setup() {
  byte ret_low, ret_high;
  unsigned short funaddr;

  Serial.begin(9600);
  asm volatile (
    "call 1f      \n\t"
    "jmp   2f     \n\t"
    "1:           \n\t"
    "pop   r2     \n\t"
    "mov   %0, r2 \n\t"
    "pop   r3     \n\t"
    "mov   %1, r3 \n\t"
    "push  r3     \n\t"
    "push  r2     \n\t"
    "ret          \n\t"
    "2:           \n\t"
    : "=r" (ret_high), "=r" (ret_low)
    :
    : "r2", "r3"
  );
```

```
    Serial.print("Return address: ");
    Serial.print(ret_high, HEX);
    Serial.println(ret_low, HEX);

    funaddr = (unsigned short) setup;
    Serial.print("Function address: ");
    Serial.println(funaddr, HEX);
}

void loop() {
}
```

The `call` instruction pushes the return address onto the stack, and then the program continues at label 1. There, the code does something that you wouldn't normally do in a function. It pops the return address off the stack; first the high byte and then the low byte. After each `pop`, it copies the value to a C/C++ variable. Then, it pushes the values right back onto the stack again. Everything is restored, and we can return from the function with `ret`, but we also have the return address available in the local variables so we can print it. The `ret` instruction pops the return address off the stack, and then the program continues at that address—the line `jmp 2f`. The last thing it does is print the return address, and the address of the `setup()` function:

```
Return address: 1F1
Function address: 1C4
```

Here's the disassembly of the relevant parts of the sketch:

```
<setup>:
388:    2f 92           push    r2
38a:    3f 92           push    r3
38c:    cf 93           push    r28
38e:    df 93           push    r29
 .
 .
 .
3de:    0e 94 f3 01     call    0x3e6
3e2:    0c 94 fa 01     jmp     0x3f4
3e6:    2f 90           pop     r2
3e8:    d2 2d           mov     r29, r2
```

```
3ea:    3f 90       pop     r3
3ec:    c3 2d       mov     r28, r3
3ee:    3f 92       push    r3
3f0:    2f 92       push    r2
3f2:    08 95       ret
```

The addresses in the leftmost column aren't the same as those printed by the sketch. To understand why we'll do a few calculations. The `setup()` function starts at 0x388 in the disassembly, and the return address is 0x3e2 (where "`jmp 0x3f4`" is located). The distance between them is 0x3e2 − 0x388 = 0x5a = 90 bytes. Compare that to the addresses printed by the sketch. The `setup()` function address there is 0x1c4 and the return address is 0x1f1. The difference is 0x1f1 − 0x1c4 = 0x2d = 45 bytes, which is exactly half of the distance in the disassembly. How can that be? I've mentioned before that all the instructions (except `jmp` and `call`) are encoded using 16 bits. Because the smallest opcode size is 16 bits, the microcontroller's Program Counter doesn't count bytes, but 16-bit words. The addresses printed by the sketch originate from the Program Counter, while the addresses in the disassembly have byte granularity. Therefore, the distances are 90 and 45 (half of 90), the `setup()` function starts at 0x388 and 0x1c4 (half of 0x388), and the return address is 0x3e2 and 0x1f1 (half of 0x3e2).

Chapter 11.
Functions

There's more than one way to use assembly code in functions. You've already seen examples of C/C++ functions with an asm statement in the middle of C/C++ code. Another type is a **C stub function**, which is exemplified by this sketch:

```
void stub_function()
{
  asm volatile (
    "nop  \n\t"
    :
    :
    :
  );
}

void setup() {
  stub_function();
}

void loop() {
```

}

A C stub function contains an `asm` statement, but no C/C++ code apart from an optional `return` statement and local variable definitions. Still, a C stub function is a regular C/C++ function where you voluntarily limit yourself a bit.

I showed you yet another type when I explained function return addresses in the last chapter. It looked like this:

```
asm volatile (
    "call 1f         \n\t"
    "jmp  2f         \n\t"
    "1:              \n\t"
    "pop  r2         \n\t"
    "mov  %0, r2     \n\t"
    "pop  r3         \n\t"
    "mov  %1, r3     \n\t"
    "push r3         \n\t"
    "push r2         \n\t"
    "ret             \n\t"
    "2:              \n\t"
    : "=r" (ret_high), "=r" (ret_low)
    :
    : "r2", "r3"
);
```

That function doesn't return a value or take any arguments, so we could argue that it's not appropriate to call it a function. The general assembly language programming term for any code that's the target of a `call` instruction—function or not—is a **subroutine**. Either way, this is one possible way of using assembly code inside a function-like construct.

Pure Assembly Functions Called From C/C++ Code

You can also create functions in pure assembly code that you can then call from C/C++ code. Here's one way to do it:

```
extern "C" byte pure_asm_inc(byte b1);

asm (
  "pure_asm_inc:   \n\t"
  "inc   r24      \n\t"
  "clr   r25      \n\t"
  "ret            \n\t"
);

void setup() {
  byte number = 3;

  Serial.begin(9600);
  Serial.print("Before increment: ");
  Serial.println(number);
  number = pure_asm_inc(3);
  Serial.print("After increment: ");
  Serial.println(number);
}

void loop() {
}
```

The function isn't *defined* but instead *declared* in C/C++ code. Then we have a **file-level** basic `asm` statement, which means that it's not located inside any other code. If we try to use an extended `asm` statement instead, we get a compilation error:

```
error: expected ')' before ':' token
```

The function `pure_asm_inc` takes one byte-sized argument. We've already covered how byte-sized arguments are passed to a function, but a bit of repetition won't hurt. The **function calling convention** is to pass arguments from left to right in the registers `r25` to `r8`. All arguments are aligned to start in even-numbered registers for optimization purposes, which means that our byte-sized argument has an unused register above it. That's why the argument is located in `r24` instead of `r25`.

What about the return value of the function? The convention is that an 8-bit return value is passed in r24, a 16-bit one in r25:r24, a 32-bit one in r22-r25, and a 64-bit one in r18-r25. We can just increment the value in r24 with the inc instruction since r24 represents both the function argument and the return value in this particular case. We clear the r25 register because the convention says that we must always extend 8-bit return values to 16 bits.

The output is what we expect:

```
Before increment: 3
After increment: 4
```

Another way to create a pure assembly function is with the **naked attribute**. It tells the compiler not to add any instructions beyond those in the basic asm statement that we put inside. With the naked attribute, we're not allowed to use the extended asm statement or any C/C++ code in the function. Adding an extended asm statement doesn't lead to a compilation error, but the result will be unreliable according to the GCC AVR documentation. I will show you why later. Here's an example of using the naked attribute:

```
byte __attribute__((naked)) pure_asm_inc(byte b1)
{
  asm (
    "inc    r24          \n\t"
    "clr    r25          \n\t"
    "ret                 \n\t"
  );
}

void setup() {
  byte number = 3;

  Serial.begin(9600);
  Serial.print("Before increment: ");
  Serial.println(number);
  number = pure_asm_inc(3);
  Serial.print("After increment: ");
  Serial.println(number);
}
```

```
void loop() {
}
```

Once again, the output is what we expect:

```
Before increment: 3
After increment: 4
```

When a C/C++ Function Calls Another C/C++ Function

There's plenty of code in the following pages, and it's not there as page filler. I'm going to show you how the compiler handles local variables and function parameters when a C/C++ function calls another C/C++ function. The `setup()` function of the sketch below assigns random numbers to 20 different local variables and prints the values one by one. In the middle of all that, it also calls another function: `level2()`. That function does the same thing as the first one, except it *doesn't* call another function in turn.

```
void __attribute__((noinline)) level2() {
  byte q1, q2, q3, q4, q5, q6, q7, q8, q9, q10, q11, q12,
      q13, q14, q15, q16, q17, q18, q19, q20;

  q1 = random();
  q2 = random();
  q3 = random();
  q4 = random();
  q5 = random();
  q6 = random();
  q7 = random();
  q8 = random();
  q9 = random();
  q10 = random();
  q11 = random();
  q12 = random();
  q13 = random();
  q14 = random();
  q15 = random();
```

```
  q16 = random();
  q17 = random();
  q18 = random();
  q19 = random();
  q20 = random();

  Serial.print(q1);
  Serial.print(q2);
  Serial.print(q3);
  Serial.print(q4);
  Serial.print(q5);
  Serial.print(q6);
  Serial.print(q7);
  Serial.print(q8);
  Serial.print(q9);
  Serial.print(q10);
  Serial.print(q11);
  Serial.print(q12);
  Serial.print(q13);
  Serial.print(q14);
  Serial.print(q15);
  Serial.print(q16);
  Serial.print(q17);
  Serial.print(q18);
  Serial.print(q19);
  Serial.print(q20);
}

void setup() {
  byte q1, q2, q3, q4, q5, q6, q7, q8, q9, q10, q11, q12,
     q13, q14, q15, q16, q17, q18, q19, q20;

  Serial.begin(9600);
  randomSeed(analogRead(0));
  q1 = random();
  q2 = random();
  q3 = random();
  q4 = random();
  q5 = random();
  q6 = random();
  q7 = random();
```

```
    q8 = random();
    q9 = random();
    q10 = random();
    q11 = random();
    q12 = random();
    q13 = random();
    q14 = random();
    q15 = random();
    q16 = random();
    q17 = random();
    q18 = random();
    q19 = random();
    q20 = random();

    level2();

    Serial.print(q1);
    Serial.print(q2);
    Serial.print(q3);
    Serial.print(q4);
    Serial.print(q5);
    Serial.print(q6);
    Serial.print(q7);
    Serial.print(q8);
    Serial.print(q9);
    Serial.print(q10);
    Serial.print(q11);
    Serial.print(q12);
    Serial.print(q13);
    Serial.print(q14);
    Serial.print(q15);
    Serial.print(q16);
    Serial.print(q17);
    Serial.print(q18);
    Serial.print(q19);
    Serial.print(q20);
}

void loop() {
}
```

Now we're going to look at the disassembly of the compiled sketch. It starts with the `setup()` function, and you can see how `random()` is called over and over again. Each time, the return value is copied into a local variable. First, the compiler uses the registers `r2` to `r17`, and then it puts the rest of the local variables on the stack using the `y` pointer register pair. Finally, the code in the `setup()` function calls the `level2()` function.

.
.
.

```
call    0x926    ; <random>
mov     r2, r22
call    0x926    ; <random>
mov     r3, r22
call    0x926    ; <random>
mov     r4, r22
call    0x926    ; <random>
mov     r5, r22
call    0x926    ; <random>
mov     r6, r22
call    0x926    ; <random>
mov     r7, r22
call    0x926    ; <random>
mov     r8, r22
call    0x926    ; <random>
mov     r9, r22
call    0x926    ; <random>
mov     r10, r22
call    0x926    ; <random>
mov     r11, r22
call    0x926    ; <random>
mov     r12, r22
call    0x926    ; <random>
mov     r13, r22
call    0x926    ; <random>
mov     r14, r22
call    0x926    ; <random>
mov     r15, r22
call    0x926    ; <random>
mov     r16, r22
```

```
call    0x926   ; <random>
mov     r17, r22
call    0x926   ; <random>
std     Y+4, r22
call    0x926   ; <random>
std     Y+3, r22
call    0x926   ; <random>
std     Y+2, r22
call    0x376   ; <level2>
```

Here's the disassembly of the `level2()` function:

```
0x376 <level2>:
push    r2
push    r3
push    r4
push    r5
push    r6
push    r7
push    r8
push    r9
push    r10
push    r11
push    r12
push    r13
push    r14
push    r15
push    r16
push    r17
push    r28
push    r29
.
.
.
call    0x926   ; <random>
mov     r2, r22
call    0x926   ; <random>
mov     r3, r22
call    0x926   ; <random>
mov     r4, r22
call    0x926   ; <random>
```

```
mov     r5, r22
call    0x926       ; <random>
mov     r6, r22
call    0x926       ; <random>
mov     r7, r22
call    0x926       ; <random>
mov     r8, r22
call    0x926       ; <random>
mov     r9, r22
call    0x926       ; <random>
mov     r10, r22
call    0x926       ; <random>
mov     r11, r22
call    0x926       ; <random>
mov     r12, r22
call    0x926       ; <random>
mov     r13, r22
call    0x926       ; <random>
mov     r14, r22
call    0x926       ; <random>
mov     r15, r22
call    0x926       ; <random>
mov     r16, r22
call    0x926       ; <random>
mov     r17, r22
call    0x926       ; <random>
std     Y+4, r22
call    0x926       ; <random>
std     Y+3, r22
call    0x926       ; <random>
std     Y+1, r22
call    0x926       ; <random>
std     Y+2, r22
mov     r24, r2
.
.
.
```

The level2() function starts by pushing the registers r2 to r17, as well as r28 and r29, onto the stack. In case you've forgotten, the y register is r29:r28. Here, it's used to reach the local variables on the stack. When it's set to a new value for use by the current function, the old value must be saved first, and that's why `r28` and `r29` are pushed onto the stack. All this housekeeping before the "real" code begins is called the **function prologue**. The opposite, where the pushed registers are restored at the end of the function, is called the **function epilogue**. After the function prologue, the code calls `random()` over and over again and copies the return values into `r2` to `r17` in the same manner as the `setup()` function did. The rest of the local variables are put on the stack this time too.

The compiler only uses as many of the registers from `r2` to `r17` as it needs for the local variables. Only the registers that are used are pushed onto the stack in the function prologue. The same principles apply if there are any function parameters—they too are allocated from the registers `r2` to `r17`. It's important to differentiate between function parameters and function arguments. C/C++ function *arguments* are passed in the registers `r25` to `r8` (left to right), but as they are copied to function *parameters*, the registers `r2` to `r17` are used.

The compiler also uses other registers than `r2` to `r17` for temporary storage. The following code comes from a modified version of the sketch above, where I've passed the random numbers as arguments to the `level2()` function:

```
ldd     r25, Y+32
std     Y+1, r25
ldd     r25, Y+33
std     Y+2, r25
ldd     r25, Y+34
std     Y+3, r25
```

The function arguments are copied to the function parameters with the `r25` register used as an intermediate. On the one hand, we have local variables and parameters stored in `r2` to `r17`. On the other hand, we have some other registers that are used for temporary storage, like `r25` above.

When a C/C++ Function Contains an Extended asm Statement, Part 1

An extended asm statement can have input and output operands. We're going to try another sketch to figure out how the compiler assigns those operands to different registers:

```
void setup() {
  byte io1=1, io2=2, io3=3, io4=4, io5=5, io6=6;
  byte oo1, oo2, oo3, oo4, oo5, oo6;

  asm volatile (
    "mov   %0, %6    \n\t"
    "mov   %1, %7    \n\t"
    "mov   %2, %8    \n\t"
    "mov   %3, %9    \n\t"
    "mov   %4, %10   \n\t"
    "mov   %5, %11   \n\t"
      : "=r" (oo1), "=r" (oo2), "=r" (oo3), "=r" (oo4),
  "=r"        (oo5), "=r" (oo6)
      : "r" (io1), "r" (io2), "r" (io3), "r" (io4), "r"
(io5),       "r" (io6)
      :
  );
  Serial.begin(9600);
  Serial.println(oo1);
  Serial.println(oo2);
  Serial.println(oo3);
  Serial.println(oo4);
  Serial.println(oo5);
  Serial.println(oo6);
}

void loop() {
}
```

First, have a look at the output:

1
2

```
3
1
5
6
```

There's something strange going on here. It should have been 1 2 3 **4** 5 6, but instead, it's 1 2 3 **1** 5 6. Let's take a detour to figure out what caused this bug.

Earlyclobber Operands

When we disassemble the compiled code, we find that the compiler has turned the `asm` statement into the following:

```
ldi     r18, 0x02
ldi     r25, 0x06
ldi     r28, 0x05
ldi     r24, 0x04
ldi     r20, 0x03
ldi     r19, 0x01
mov     r24, r19
mov     r15, r18
mov     r16, r20
mov     r17, r24
mov     r29, r28
mov     r28, r25
```

Can you spot the error? Here's the original line we have a problem with:

```
"mov   %3, %9   \n\t"
```

It's split into two separate lines in the disassembly. First, the `io4` variable value is copied into the `r24` register, which represents the `%9` input operand:

```
ldi     r24, 0x04
```

Next, `r24` is copied to `r17`, which represents the `%3` output operand:

```
mov     r17, r24
```

Between those two lines, we have this line:

```
mov     r24, r19
```

That's where the `io1` variable value is copied to the input operand %6. It too is represented by the `r24` register, and that's what's gone wrong. There's one more rule I haven't told you about yet: *you're no longer allowed to use any of the input operands after you've written to any of the output operands*. When the compiler optimizes the code, it might use the same register to represent an input operand and an output operand. That leads to the kind of bug we've just encountered.

There's a way to break the rule and still avoid the bug. We can tell the compiler that the output operands are **earlyclobber operands**, which means that we're going to write to them before we've finished using the input operands. We use the constraint modifier & to mark an output operand as an earlyclobber operand.

When a C/C++ Function Contains an Extended asm Statement, Part 2

Here's the correct version of our previous sketch:

```
void setup() {
  byte io1=1, io2=2, io3=3, io4=4, io5=5, io6=6;
  byte oo1, oo2, oo3, oo4, oo5, oo6;

  asm volatile (
    "mov    %0, %6   \n\t"
    "mov    %1, %7   \n\t"
    "mov    %2, %8   \n\t"
    "mov    %3, %9   \n\t"
    "mov    %4, %10  \n\t"
    "mov    %5, %11  \n\t"
    : "=&r" (oo1), "=&r" (oo2), "=&r" (oo3), "=&r" (oo4),
      "=&r" (oo5), "=&r" (oo6)
    : "r" (io1), "r" (io2), "r" (io3), "r" (io4), "r" (io5),
      "r" (io6)
    :
```

```
    );
    Serial.begin(9600);
    Serial.println(oo1);
    Serial.println(oo2);
    Serial.println(oo3);
    Serial.println(oo4);
    Serial.println(oo5);
    Serial.println(oo6);
}

void loop() {
}
```

This time the output is what we expect:

```
1
2
3
4
5
6
```

Let's take a look at the disassembly again:

```
ldi     r18, 0x02
ldi     r25, 0x06
ldi     r22, 0x05
ldi     r21, 0x04
ldi     r20, 0x03
ldi     r19, 0x01
mov     r24, r19
mov     r15, r18
mov     r16, r20
mov     r17, r21
mov     r29, r22
mov     r28, r25
```

In this particular example, the compiler used the registers r15-r22, r24-r25, and r28-r29 for the input and output operands. No input operand registers were reused for the output operands since we applied the & constraint modifier.

Call-Used and Call-Saved Registers

There's a convention that divides the general-purpose registers into the **call-used registers** (r18-r27 and r30-r31) and the **call-saved registers** (r2-r17 and r28-r29). We've already seen that the compiler uses r2-r17 to store local variables and function parameters. Now we can restate that: the compiler uses the call-saved registers to store local variables and parameters. We've also seen that the prologue of a C/C++ function pushes all the call-saved registers it's going to use onto the stack and that the epilogue restores them before the function returns.

Finally, we saw an example of the compiler using the registers r15-r22, r24-r25, and r28-r29 for the input and output operands of an extended asm statement. That's a mix of call-used and call-saved registers.

I've already shown you two different ways to call a pure assembly function from a C/C++ function. As I pointed out then, you *must* use a basic asm statement in both cases. That way there will never be any input or output operands, and therefore the compiler will never put any call-used registers (r18-r27 and r30-r31) in the code. *You* might be using some of them in *your own* assembly code, and you're free to use any call-used register any way you like. If you break the rules and use an extended asm statement with the naked attribute, it doesn't lead to a compilation error, but there may be a collision if the compiler assigns a call-used register to any of the input or output operands. That's why the GCC AVR documentation states that the result will be unreliable.

If C/C++ code calls your pure assembly function, it's up to the compiler to make sure that there will be no collisions with the call-used registers (r18-r27 and r30-r31). That's why I've mentioned temporary use of the call-used registers in C/C++ code. The compiler might, for example, generate a couple of instructions that use one of the registers, be done with it, and then call your pure assembly code. If the compiler needs the values to be preserved past the call, it must save them before it calls your function and restore them afterward.

If you use any of the call-saved registers (r2-r17 and r28-r29) in your pure assembly function, you *must* save and restore them on behalf of the calling function. The same thing happens automatically in the prologue of a C/C++ function when the call-saved registers are pushed onto the stack. Because it's not done automatically in a pure assembly function, you must do it yourself. On the other hand, if you call a C/C++ function *from* your pure assembly function, you don't have to worry about the call-saved registers as the function will save and restore them for you. The C/C++ function won't save the call-used registers (r18-r27 and r30-r31) though, and might clobber them, for example when it uses them for temporary storage.

Since function arguments are passed in the registers r25 to r8, both call-used and call-saved registers are involved. The call-used rules apply for r25 to r18, and the call-saved rules apply for r17 to r8.

A Repeated Warning About the Call-Used Registers

I warned you about the call-used registers early in the book, but at the time I wasn't able to put it in context. The free use of the call-used registers (r18-r27 and r30-r31) in assembly code *doesn't* apply to asm statements inside C/C++ functions. You *must* use the clobber list to specify any registers you clobber there, including the call-used registers. It's *only* in pure assembly functions that you can use these registers freely without saving and restoring them.

Chapter 12.
Logic, Shift and Rotate Instructions

Logic Instructions

I'm not going to explain the absolute basics of the logic instructions, because I assume that you have a good grasp of the bitwise operators in C/C++ (&, |, ^, ~, <<, and >>). The logic instructions in AVR assembly are: `and`, `andi` (and with a constant), `or`, `ori` (or with a constant), `eor` (xor) and `com` (not, inverse, or one's complement). They're used with registers and constants, like so:

```
and   r2, r3
andi  r16, 0x55
or    r2, r3
ori   r16, 0x55
eor   r2, r3
com   r2
```

A **bitmask** or **mask** is a binary number that you can use to modify another binary number with the help of the logic instructions. If you want to set one or more bits, you use a mask where the corresponding bits are already set, and then you `or` both numbers. If you want to clear one or more bits, you use a mask where the corresponding bits are already cleared, and then you `and` both numbers. Finally, if you want to toggle one or more bits (change 0s to 1s and 1s to 0s), you use a mask where the corresponding bits are set, and then you `eor` both numbers.

Leftward Shift and Rotate Instructions

There are two different instructions that move all the bits of a register one step to the left. Both move the leftmost bit into the Carry Flag, but the difference between them is what is moved into the rightmost bit. The `lsl` (**logical shift left**) instruction clears bit 0, while the `rol` (**rotate left through carry**) instruction moves the old Carry Flag value into bit 0. The Carry Flag is involved twice with the `rol` instruction, and that is what makes it a rotating one. Run `rol` nine times in a row, and you're back where you started:

```
76543210    C
6543210C    7       (1)
543210C7    6       (2)
43210C76    5       (3)
3210C765    4       (4)
210C7654    3       (5)
10C76543    2       (6)
0C765432    1       (7)
C7654321    0       (8)
76543210    C       (9)
```

The numbers above are the original bit numbers, and C is the original Carry Flag value. The middle column is the Carry Flag value at each step. The numbers in parenthesis are the number of times the `rol` instruction has executed.

The `lsl` instruction multiplies numbers by two. It works equally well on both signed and unsigned numbers. Since we haven't yet looked at how signed numbers are stored, we'll have to make do with an unsigned example. We're going to double the number 105, which is 0110 1001 in binary. We shift it once to the left, bringing in a zero at bit position 0, and get 1101 0010, which is 210 in decimal.

The idea behind this method is that the bit position directly to the left of another bit position is worth twice as much. The right-most position is worth 1, the next one 2, then 4, 8, 16, 32, 64, and 128. If a bit is set and moves one step to the left, its value doubles, and when all the bits in the byte move one step to the left, the whole byte value doubles. The left-most bit moves to the Carry Flag, which therefore gets set if the result is bigger than what can be stored in one byte.

We can double a 16-bit number by running the `rol` instruction straight after the `lsl` instruction. The left-most bit from the lower byte now moves—via the Carry Flag—to the right-most bit of the higher byte. Then, all the bits of the higher byte move one step to the left, and the left-most bit moves to the Carry Flag. We can run the `rol` instruction again a couple of times if we wish to double a 32-bit number instead.

Here's a sketch that demonstrates this method by multiplying 13209 by two:

```
volatile __attribute__((used)) uint16_t u1 = 13209, u2;

void setup() {
  asm volatile (
    "mov    r15, %A1    \n\t"
    "mov    r16, %B1    \n\t"
    "lsl    r15         \n\t"
    "rol    r16         \n\t"
    "mov    %A0, r15    \n\t"
    "mov    %B0, r16    \n\t"
    : "=r" (u2)
    : "r" (u1)
    : "r15", "r16"
  );
  Serial.begin(9600);
  Serial.print("u2=");
  Serial.println(u2);
}

void loop() {
}
```

As expected, it prints:

u2=26418

Rightward Shift and Rotate Instructions

While moving all the bits one step to the left doubles an unsigned value, moving them one step to the right divides by two. The idea behind this method is that the bit position directly to the right of another bit position is worth half as much.

There's an instruction called `lsr` (**logical shift right**) that moves all the bits one step to the right, clears bit 7 and moves bit 0 to the Carry Flag. You can use it on a single byte-sized value, or you can use it on the highest byte of a multi-byte value. If you work with a multi-byte value, you use one or more `ror` (**rotate right through carry**) instructions afterward. The `ror` instruction moves all the bits one step to the right, puts the old Carry Flag value in bit 7 and moves bit 0 to the Carry Flag. The final Carry Flag value is the remainder of the division.

There's a third instruction called `asr` (**arithmetic shift right**) that works with signed numbers. I'll cover it when we get to how signed numbers are stored, in the chapter about arithmetic instructions.

Chapter 13.
Interrupts

When an **interrupt** occurs, the microcontroller stops executing whatever it's executing at the time and continues at the appropriate **interrupt handler** instead. An interrupt handler is also called an **interrupt service routine**, or an **interrupt routine**.

Using Interrupts to Blink the Debug LED

To explore how interrupts work, we'll look at a sketch that blinks the debug LED rapidly:

```
asm (
  ".global __vector_13   \n\t"
  "__vector_13:          \n\t"

  "push r16              \n\t"
  "push r17              \n\t"
  "in   r16, __SREG__    \n\t"
  "push r16              \n\t"

  "ldi  r16, 0b00100000  \n\t"
```

```
        "in    r17, 0x05             \n\t"
        "eor   r16, r17              \n\t"
        "out   0x05, r16             \n\t"

        "pop   r16                   \n\t"
        "out   __SREG__, r16         \n\t"
        "pop   r17                   \n\t"
        "pop   r16                   \n\t"

        "reti                        \n\t"
);

void setup() {
  asm (
    "ldi r16, 0b00100000       \n\t"
    "out 0x04, r16             \n\t"

    "ldi xl, 0x80              \n\t"
    "ldi xh, 0x00              \n\t"

    "st   x+, __zero_reg__     \n\t"
    "ldi r16, 2                \n\t"
    "st   x+, r16              \n\t"
    "st   x, __zero_reg__      \n\t"

    "ldi xl, 0x6f              \n\t"
    "ldi xh, 0x00              \n\t"
    "ldi r16, 1                \n\t"
    "st   x, r16               \n\t"
    : : : "r16"
  );
}

void loop() {
}
```

The `setup()` function sets the direction of the pin the debug LED is connected to:

```
"ldi r16, 0b00100000       \n\t"
"out 0x04, r16             \n\t"
```

It also contains code that initializes the 16-bit Timer/Counter 1. Exactly how the timers work aren't important for our purposes, and I've tried to simplify that part of the code as much as possible. The following five lines make the timer tick with 1/8 of the clock frequency (which is 16 MHz on both the Arduino Uno and the Arduino Mega 2560):

```
"ldi  xl, 0x80              \n\t"
"ldi  xh, 0x00              \n\t"
"st   x+, __zero_reg__      \n\t"
"ldi  r16, 2                \n\t"
"st   x+, r16               \n\t"
"st   x, __zero_reg__       \n\t"
```

That means one tick every 500 nanoseconds. Since the timer is 16-bit, it takes 2^16=65536 ticks for it to overflow, which means that it overflows every 65536 * 500 nanoseconds, or roughly 30 times a second. The timer counts from 0 to 65535 and then overflows back to 0 again. We're going to let the LED switch state at every overflow, so it takes two overflows to produce one blink cycle, which makes the LED blink about 15 times a second.

Only the timer overflowing won't make the LED blink. We need some more initialization code:

```
"ldi  xl, 0x6f              \n\t"
"ldi  xh, 0x00              \n\t"
"ldi  r16, 1                \n\t"
"st   x, r16                \n\t"
```

The x register is loaded to point to 0x006f, which is the address of a register called TIMSK1 (Timer/Counter 1 Interrupt Mask). Bit 0 of that register is the Overflow Interrupt Enable bit, and when we set it, an interrupt called TIMER1 OVF is generated each time the timer overflows.

TIMER1 OVF has a corresponding **interrupt vector** in the flash program memory. It consists of two 16-bit words that are executed each time the interrupt occurs, and the words contain the instruction jmp and a destination address. The interrupt vectors for all the different interrupts are stored in a table in the flash memory, starting at address 0x0000. The interrupt vector number for TIMER1 OVF is 14 (1-based) or 13 (0-based). Because each interrupt vector consists of two 16-bit words, which equals four bytes, the 0-based interrupt vector number 13 starts at the byte address 4 * 13 = 52 in the table. The program counter counts 16-bit words instead of bytes, so the actual address isn't 52, but instead 52 / 2 = 26 = 0x001a. When the TIMER1 OVF interrupt is generated because of a timer overflow, the microcontroller executes the instructions starting at address 0x001a. We must make the interrupt vector at address 0x001a point to our interrupt handler. The compiler solves that for us automatically if we provide it with the following lines:

```
asm (
  ".global __vector_13   \n\t"
  "__vector_13:          \n\t"
```

The compiler points the `jmp` to `__vector_13`, which is the label where our interrupt handler starts. The `.global` directive makes the symbol visible to the linker.

The code that follows is the interrupt handler. When it starts executing, some other code has been interrupted while it was running. That code will malfunction when it continues running a bit later if our interrupt handler writes haphazardly to various registers. We must push the registers we are going to use to the stack—but not only those. Imagine that a comparison instruction was the last one to execute before the interrupt and that the next instruction is a branch instruction. Then the branch instruction won't work properly if the interrupt handler has changed the SREG flags. We must push the SREG to the stack, too. All that is accomplished by the following instructions:

```
"push r16              \n\t"
"push r17              \n\t"
"in   r16, __SREG__    \n\t"
"push r16              \n\t"
```

While we're at it, we can as well look at the instructions that restore the state at the end of the interrupt handler. Notice how the order is the opposite, as the stack works in a LIFO fashion:

```
"pop    r16             \n\t"
"out    __SREG__, r16   \n\t"
"pop    r17             \n\t"
"pop    r16             \n\t"
```

Between the save and restore instructions are the instructions that do the actual interrupt handling:

```
"ldi    r16, 0b00100000 \n\t"
"in     r17, 0x05       \n\t"
"eor    r16, r17        \n\t"
"out    0x05, r16       \n\t"
```

All they do is invert the bit that controls the pin connected to the debug LED. The `eor` instruction is the xor instruction of the AVR, and to xor with 1 makes a 1 become a 0, and a 0 become a 1.

The final instruction of the interrupt handler is `reti`. It pops the return address from the stack, continues the execution there, and sets the global interrupt flag.

The Global Interrupt Flag

SREG bit 7 is called Global Interrupt Enable, or the **global interrupt flag**. Clearing it disables all interrupts. When an interrupt occurs, the microcontroller clears that flag automatically. The `reti` instruction at the end of the interrupt handler sets it again. You can also set and clear the flag using the `sei` and `cli` instructions. If you set it inside your interrupt handler, you're allowing other interrupts to interrupt your interrupt handler—a situation called **nested interrupts**. Most of the time you won't need nested interrupts, and then you can rely on the default behavior instead.

A Warning About the Zero Register in Interrupt Handlers

There's one more small, but crucial, detail that you must know about. Imagine that some code has changed the content of `r1` to something other than zero, and then an interrupt occurs. A situation where that can happen is straight after a `mul` (multiplication) instruction, where the result is put in `r0` and `r1`. If we use `r1` in our interrupt handler and assume that it contains zero, we're going to have a bug that could be difficult to troubleshoot. Therefore, we must always clear the `r1` register before we use it as the zero register in an interrupt handler consisting of pure assembly code. Sometimes the compiler helps you with the `r1` register, and I'll describe those cases later.

Macros for Interrupt Handlers

What I've shown you so far is a pure assembly interrupt handler. Usually, you would use a macro to define the interrupt handler instead. Here's a pure assembly skeleton for comparison:

```
asm (
  ".global __vector_13   \n\t"
  "__vector_13:          \n\t"
    .
    .
    .
  "reti   \n\t"
);
```

Here's the same interrupt handler, but this time it's defined with the `ISR` (Interrupt Service Routine) macro:

```
ISR(TIMER1_OVF_vect, ISR_NAKED)
{
  asm (
    .
    .
    .
    "reti   \n\t"
  );
}
```

Instead of specifying the interrupt vector with a number, we define it using the constant `TIMER1_OVF_vect`. We use the `ISR_NAKED` attribute to ensure that the compiler doesn't insert any code beyond the one in our asm statement. If we want the compiler to add a prologue and an epilogue to the interrupt handler, we can use the `ISR_BLOCK` attribute instead of `ISR_NAKED`. Here's a disassembly where only the prologue and epilogue are shown:

```
push    r1
push    r0
in      r0, 0x3f
push    r0
eor     r1, r1
.
.
.
pop     r0
out     0x3f, r0
pop     r0
pop     r1
reti
```

The compiler doesn't save and restore all the registers that we use—only `r0`, `r1`, and `SREG`. It also makes sure that the `r1` register is zero when the actual interrupt handler code starts. It does so by xoring r1 with itself.

If you want the global interrupt flag to be set when the interrupt handler starts, you can use the attribute `ISR_NOBLOCK` instead of `ISR_BLOCK`.

Interrupt Vector Names

There's a list of all the interrupt vectors in the datasheets for the ATmega328P and ATmega2560 microcontrollers. The interrupt vector names used by the ISR macro look slightly different. Take the name from the list in the datasheets, remove everything but the letters and numbers, and replace the spaces with underscores. Then add _vect at the end.

The Timer/Counter 1 overflow interrupt is called TIMER1 OVF in the datasheet lists. There are no non-alphanumeric characters to remove, but we must replace the space with an underscore. Finally, we add _vect at the end and get `TIMER1_OVF_vect`, which we can use with the `ISR` macro.

Chapter 14.
Assembly Files

In the previous chapter, we studied a sketch that utilized a timer and interrupts to blink the debug LED. In this chapter, we'll change that sketch from using inline assembly to using an **assembly file**. That's a file with no C/C++ code in it at all.

The C/C++ part of the Arduino sketch is new:

```
extern "C" {
  void prepare();
  void __vector_13();
}

void setup() {
  prepare();
}

void loop() {
}
```

The assembly code from the `setup()` function can now be found in the `prepare()` function instead. It's declared in the C/C++ code, but the actual function is in the assembly file. The declaration of the interrupt handler __vector_13() works the same way.

To add an assembly file to the sketch, you click on the small downward-pointing black arrow in the upper right corner of the Arduino IDE. Select New Tab, and enter a filename for the new file. Make sure to end the filename with the .S extension (an upper-case S).

The .S file in our example looks like this:

```
.global __vector_13
.global prepare

__SREG__ = 0x3f
__zero_reg__ = 1

__vector_13:

    push  r16
    push  r17
    in    r16, __SREG__
    push  r16

    ldi   r16, 0b00100000
    in    r17, 0x05
    eor   r16, r17
    out   0x05, r16

    pop   r16
    out   __SREG__, r16
    pop   r17
    pop   r16

    reti

prepare:

    ldi r18, 0b00100000
    out 0x04, r18
```

```
ldi xl, 0x80
ldi xh, 0x00

st  x+, __zero_reg__
ldi r18, 2
st  x+, r18
st  x, __zero_reg__

ldi xl, 0x6f
ldi xh, 0x00
ldi r18, 1
st  x, r18

ret
```

The code is very similar to the code in the previous chapter, but there are no quotation marks around the lines as in inline assembly and no \n\t sequences. Because this is an assembly file, we can't use __SREG__ and __zero_reg__ as we can in inline assembly code without defining them first, like so:

```
__SREG__ = 0x3f
__zero_reg__ = 1
```

The prepare() function uses r18, while the original sketch used r16 for the same purpose. When the code was in an extended asm statement, we could put r16 in the clobber list. In an assembly file, there's no clobber list to put it in, so we use the call-used register r18 instead. We could have used the call-saved r16 register here too, but then we would have had to push and pop it to save and restore it.

Chapter 15.
Arithmetic and Logic Instructions

Accessing Global Variables

Before we begin with the arithmetic and logic instructions, I want to show you an easy way to access variables from inline assembly code. You don't always have to use input and output operands. If the variable is global, you can access it without further ado. Here's a sketch that illustrates how:

```
volatile __attribute__((used)) uint8_t u = 9;

void setup() {
  Serial.begin(9600);
  Serial.println(u);
  asm volatile (
    "lds   r2, u    \n\t"
    "inc   r2       \n\t"
    "sts   u, r2    \n\t"
    :
    :
    : "r2"
  );
```

```
    Serial.println(u);
}

void loop() {
}
```

Making the u variable `volatile` tells the compiler that something else than the C/C++ code might modify it. The compiler must make sure that the compiled code reads the value from the u variable each time it's used, instead of relying on a value it might have stored temporarily somewhere else for optimization purposes. To ensure that the compiler doesn't optimize the variable away even though it's not referenced anywhere, we also need `__attribute__((used))`. The compiler can't see that we use the variable because it doesn't understand the assembly code. Finally, there's a new instruction in the sketch: `lds` (**load direct from data space**) copies the byte from the address specified by u to the `r2` register.

Incrementing and Decrementing

To add one to a register, you use the `inc` instruction:

```
inc    r22
```

You can also subtract one with the `dec` instruction:

```
dec    r22
```

Two's Complement

I'm going to demonstrate how both unsigned and signed numbers can be stored in the general-purpose registers. Here's a sketch that does some copying back and forth:

```
volatile __attribute__((used)) uint8_t u;
volatile __attribute__((used)) int8_t i1 = -10, i2;

void setup() {
  asm volatile (
```

```
    "lds   r15, i1     \n\t"
    "sts   u, r15      \n\t"
    "sts   i2, r15     \n\t"
    :
    :
    : "r15"
  );
  Serial.begin(9600);
  Serial.print("u=");
  Serial.println(u);
  Serial.print("i2=");
  Serial.println(i2);
}

void loop() {
}
```

We assign -10 to the signed 8-bit variable `i1`. Then we copy `i1` to the `r15` register and `r15` to the unsigned 8-bit variable `u`. The `r15` register is nothing more than a container for 8 bits, and it has no information about the **signedness** of the number it contains—that is, whether the number is signed or unsigned. By printing u, we can figure out what bit pattern `r15` contains after we copy -10 into it. Finally, we also copy `r15` to the signed 8-bit variable `i2`. Is the value -10 still there when we print `i2`? Here's the result:

```
u=246
i2=-10
```

The `i2` variable contains -10 even though we stored the value temporarily in the `r15` register, without any explicit specification of its signedness. The u variable contains an entirely different value. The relationship between -10 and 246 is what's called the **two's complement**. To get the decimal number -10 in binary, we start with the decimal number 10 in binary, which is 0000 1010. Then we invert all the bits (turn 0 into 1, and 1 into 0) and get 1111 0101. Finally, we add 1 and get 1111 0110, which is the same as 246 in decimal. The general rule is: invert all the bits, add one, and throw away the carry if you get one.

The numbers -10 and 246 look the same while they are stored in r15. They are printed as -10 in one case and as 246 in the other case, because the variables i2 and u are declared as signed and unsigned, which affects how they are printed. It doesn't affect how the numbers are stored in the r15 register. The bit pattern there is 1111 0110 in both cases, and that's the bit pattern in the variables too.

Let's try a few more examples. The decimal number 1 equals 0000 0001 in binary. The two's complement of 1 is used to represent -1. We invert all the bits of 0000 0001 and get 1111 1110. Then we add 1 and get 1111 1111, which is 255 in decimal. Doing the same with the numbers 2 and -2, we get 0000 0010 and the two's complement 1111 1110 (254 in decimal). If we go a bit higher and try 127 and -127, we get 0111 1111 and the two's complement 1000 0001 (129 in decimal). The method doesn't work as well with 128 and -128. Now we get 1000 0000 and the two's complement 1000 0000 for both numbers, but we can't have one binary number representing both a positive and a negative number at the same time. The binary number 1000 0000 is defined as the decimal number -128 instead of 128.

We can store any number from -128 to 127 in one signed byte. To calculate the two's complement in assembly language, you can use the instruction neg, which replaces the content of a register with its two's complement.

Adding Signed and Unsigned Numbers

Here's an example of adding an unsigned variable and a signed variable using the add instruction:

```
volatile __attribute__((used)) uint8_t u = 10;
volatile __attribute__((used)) int8_t i1 = -7, i2;

void setup() {
  asm volatile (
    "lds  r15, u      \n\t"
    "lds  r16, i1     \n\t"
    "add  r15, r16    \n\t"
    "sts  i2, r15     \n\t"
    :
    :
```

```
    : "r15", "r16"
  );
  Serial.begin(9600);
  Serial.print("i2=");
  Serial.println(i2);
}

void loop() {
}
```

The result we get is:

`i2=3`

That's the correct answer, because 10 + (-7) = 10 − 7 = 3. What is not immediately obvious, though, is why it works with the `add` instruction and the two's complement to represent negative numbers.

Let's start with a randomly selected binary number: 1001 1100. The inverse is 0110 0011. Add them together, just like you add ordinary decimal numbers:

```
   1001 1100
 + 0110 0011
   ─────────
   1111 1111
```

If you look closely at the calculation, you will soon realize that no matter what n-bit number you take, adding its inverse always results in a new n-bit number with only ones in it. Adding 1 to such a number creates yet another number, 2^n, that is 1 bit larger than the first one because of the carry. 2^n is how many different combinations of 0s and 1s we can store in n bits. Starting at 0, the highest number we can store is 2^n-1, and 2^n is one more than that. An example is $2^8 = 256 = $ 0b 0000 0001 0000 0000.

Now we know that if we take an n-bit number, add its inverse, and then add one more, we get 2^n. That's the same as taking an n-bit number and adding its two's complement. Let's use M as the symbol for the two's complement of N. Then we know that $N + M = 2^n$. After subtracting N from both sides, we get $M = 2^n - N$. Thus, the two's complement of an n-bit binary number, N, is $2^n - N$.

Imagine that we have two n-bit binary numbers B and C. We want to calculate B − C, and we do so step by step:

$B - C = B - C + 2^n - 2^n = B + (2^n - C) - 2^n$

2^n - C is the same as the two's complement of C, while 2^n is a number that is one bigger than the biggest number we can represent with n bits. Remember the rule that we simply ignore the carry if we get one while calculating the two's complement, so we ignore the last 2^n. We're left with B plus the two's complement of C. To sum it up, B − C equals B plus the two's complement of C.

Our example sketch used the number 10 and the two's complement of 7. We've already decided that the two's complement of 7 should represent -7, but now we also know that if we add that to 10, the result is the same as 10 − 7. That's good because we want additions with the two's complement to give the mathematically correct answers.

Remember that you can use the `neg` instruction to calculate the two's complement in assembly language. The `add` instruction works with both positive and negative numbers as long as you use the two's complement to represent the negative ones. Therefore, the same `add` instruction works with both signed and unsigned numbers. You don't have to perform any of the complicated calculations that I've shown you above, but now you know why everything works so smoothly if you stick to using the two's complement.

Unsigned Carry and Signed Overflow

When I introduced the SREG a few chapters ago, I also showed how the Carry Flag works with the `add` instruction. When you `add` two registers, and the result is bigger than 255, it won't fit in the destination register. The maximum unsigned number that you can store in one byte is 255 (1111 1111 in binary). Add two of those, and you get the binary number 0000 0001 1111 1110. As you can see, you get an extra bit that doesn't fit in an 8-bit register. You can get an extra bit even with smaller numbers than those, but that's the worst case, so you can be sure that there's never more than one extra bit. It's the one that the `add` instruction puts in the Carry Flag in the SREG.

Adding signed numbers is different. A signed byte can hold a value between -128 and 127. As soon as the sum of the numbers we add is above 127, there's an **overflow**, and the **Two's Complement Overflow Flag** is set in the SREG.

Here's a sketch that calculates 126 + 1 and 126 + 2, and also prints the value of the SREG after each calculation:

```
volatile __attribute__((used)) int8_t i1=126, i2=1,
    i3 = 126, i4 = 2, result_no_overflow,
    result_overflow;
volatile __attribute__((used)) byte
    sreg_value_no_overflow, sreg_value_overflow;

void setup() {
  Serial.begin(9600);
  asm volatile (
    // Addition that doesn't set the Two's Complement
    // Overflow Flag
    "lds   r16, i1                       \n\t"
    "lds   r17, i2                       \n\t"
    "add   r16, r17                      \n\t"
    "sts   result_no_overflow, r16       \n\t"
    "in    r16, __SREG__                 \n\t"
    "sts sreg_value_no_overflow, r16   \n\t"

    // Addition that sets the Two's Complement Overflow
    // Flag
    "lds   r16, i3                       \n\t"
    "lds   r17, i4                       \n\t"
    "add   r16, r17                      \n\t"
    "sts   result_overflow, r16          \n\t"
    "in    r16, __SREG__                 \n\t"
    "sts sreg_value_overflow, r16      \n\t"

    :
    :
    : "r16", "r17"
  );
```

```
  Serial.print("Result without Two's Complement Overflow
      Flag set=");
  Serial.println(result_no_overflow);
  Serial.print("SREG without Two's Complement Overflow
      Flag set=");
  Serial.println(sreg_value_no_overflow, HEX);
  Serial.print("Result with Two's Complement Overflow
Flag set=");
  Serial.println(result_overflow);
  Serial.print("SREG with Two's Complement Overflow Flag
      set=");
  Serial.println(sreg_value_overflow, HEX);
}

void loop() {
}
```

The sketch prints this:

```
Result without Two's Complement Overflow Flag set=127
SREG without Two's Complement Overflow Flag set=80
Result with Two's Complement Overflow Flag set=-128
SREG with Two's Complement Overflow Flag set=AC
```

126 + 1 = 127, so the first result is correct, but 126 + 2 = 128 and we got -128 instead. The SREG was 0x80 with the correct answer. That's 1000 0000 in binary. I'm going to repeat what the SREG looks like because I don't expect you to remember that:

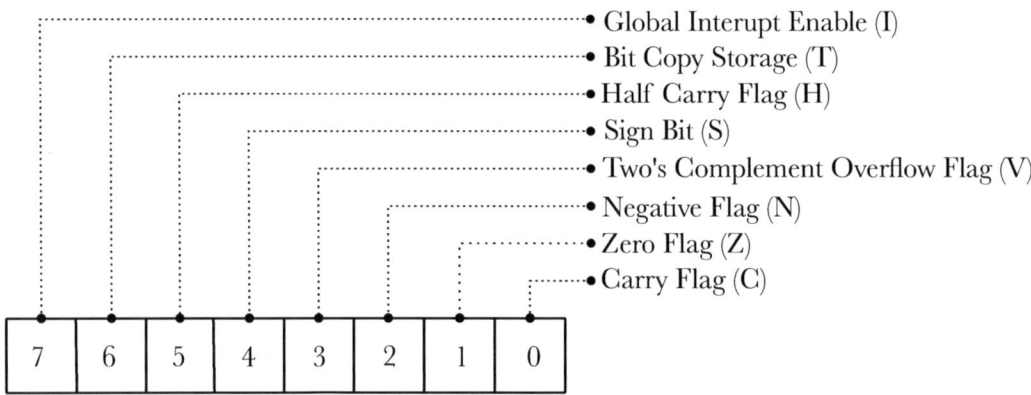

As you can see, the Two's Complement Overflow Flag was cleared. When the result was incorrect, the SREG was 0xac, which is 1010 1100 in binary. This time the Two's Complement Overflow Flag was set, because the sum of the two numbers we added was larger than the largest positive value that can be stored in one signed byte. The flag is also set if we add two negative numbers and the sum is smaller than the most negative number that can be stored in one signed byte.

Signed and Unsigned Addition with Carry

The `add` instruction only works with byte-sized values, but we can easily do 16-bit addition too with one more instruction. Here we add two negative 16-bit numbers:

```
void setup() {
  int16_t i1 = -10000, i2 = -20000, i3;

  asm volatile (
    "mov   r15, %A1   \n\t"
    "mov   r16, %B1   \n\t"
    "mov   r17, %A2   \n\t"
    "mov   r18, %B2   \n\t"
    "add   r15, r17   \n\t"
    "adc   r16, r18   \n\t"
    "mov   %A0, r15   \n\t"
    "mov   %B0, r16   \n\t"
    : "=r" (i3)
    : "r" (i1), "r" (i2)
    : "r15", "r16", "r17", "r18"
  );
  Serial.begin(9600);
  Serial.print("i3=");
  Serial.println(i3);
}

void loop() {
}
```

The result is as expected:

```
i3=-30000
```

By now, you should be able to understand the whole sketch except for this part:

```
"add   r15, r17    \n\t"
"adc   r16, r18    \n\t"
```

The first line adds the lower bytes together. The Carry Flag is set if there's a carry, and the next instruction, adc (**add with carry**), adds the higher bytes plus the Carry Flag. That way, we have a complete 16-bit addition. This method works with both signed and unsigned integers.

Subtraction with and without Carry

The subtraction equivalents of add and adc are called sub and sbc. We'll begin with a sketch as usual. This one calculates 20000 – 5000 and prints the result:

```
void setup() {
  int16_t i1 = 20000, i2 = 5000, i3;

  asm volatile (
    "mov   r15, %A1    \n\t"
    "mov   r16, %B1    \n\t"
    "mov   r17, %A2    \n\t"
    "mov   r18, %B2    \n\t"
    "sub   r15, r17    \n\t"
    "sbc   r16, r18    \n\t"
    "mov   %A0, r15    \n\t"
    "mov   %B0, r16    \n\t"
    : "=r" (i3)
    : "r" (i1), "r" (i2)
    : "r15", "r16", "r17", "r18"
  );
  Serial.begin(9600);
  Serial.print("i3=");
  Serial.println(i3);
```

```
}

void loop() {
}
```

There are no surprises when we look at what's printed:

```
i3=15000
```

The only question that remains is *why* the sketch works. If we write 20000 − 5000 = 15000 in hexadecimal we get 0x4e20 − 0x1388 = 0x3a98. The `sub` instruction calculates the difference between the lower bytes: 0x20 − 0x88 = 0x98. We can arrive at that result in two different ways.

We already know that B − C equals B plus the two's complement of C. 0x88 equals 1000 1000 in binary, and the inverse of that is 0111 0111. Add one, and we get 0111 1000, which is the same as 0x78. 0x20 + 0x78 = 0x98. The `sub` instruction has an extra feature: because 0x88 is bigger than 0x20, it sets the Carry Flag. Next, we continue with the other way to arrive at the same result.

Once again we're trying to calculate 0x20 − 0x88, but this time we want a positive result. Therefore, we **borrow** from the higher byte to 0x20. 0x4e becomes 0x4e − 1 = 0x4d, while 0x20 becomes 0x120. We subtract the lower bytes: 0x120 − 0x88 = 0x98. Then we subtract the higher bytes: 0x4d − 0x13 = 0x3a. The final result is 0x3a98 = 15000. When we run the `sub` instruction, we calculate 0x120 − 0x88 and get 0x98, but that instruction doesn't know about the `r16` and `r18` registers holding the higher bytes. Instead, it sets the Carry Flag to mark that we need to borrow one from the higher byte.

No matter which of the two ways we choose to look at it, we're now at the point where the `sub` instruction has calculated the result 0x98, and the Carry Flag is set. It's time for the instruction `sbc` (**subtract with carry**) to take over and subtract the higher bytes. Again, there are two ways to arrive at the same result.

The `sbc` instruction calculates 0x4e − 0x13, and it also subtracts the value of the Carry Flag because the documentation says so. In this case the Carry Flag is set, and the result is: 0x4e − 0x13 − 1 = 0x3a. The final result of the whole subtraction is 0x3a98 = 15000. That explanation is correct, but it doesn't help much with understanding why. Now to the second way of looking at it.

The Carry Flag has been set to mark that the `sub` instruction needed to borrow from the higher byte to get a positive result. Therefore, we don't have 0x4e left, but only 0x4e – 1 = 0x4d. The `sbc` instruction performs both that subtraction, and the next subtraction: 0x4d – 0x13 = 0x3a. The final result is, again, 0x3a98 = 15000, but this time we understand *why* we arrived at that result.

The method demonstrated in the sketch works with both signed and unsigned integers.

Arithmetic Shift Right

When I covered shift and rotate instructions in an earlier chapter, I told you that I skipped an instruction called `asr` (**arithmetic shift right**) that works with signed numbers.

Let's start with why there's no `asl` instruction in the AVR instruction set. When we double a signed number by shifting left, we can use the same instructions as with unsigned numbers. While explaining why, I'm going to surprise you a bit. Here's the sketch I used to illustrate the `lsl` and `rol` instructions:

```
void setup() {
  uint16_t u1 = 13209, u2;

  asm volatile (
    "mov   r15, %A1    \n\t"
    "mov   r16, %B1    \n\t"
    "lsl   r15         \n\t"
    "rol   r16         \n\t"
    "mov   %A0, r15    \n\t"
    "mov   %B0, r16    \n\t"
    : "=r" (u2)
    : "r" (u1)
    : "r15", "r16"
  );
```

```
    Serial.begin(9600);
    Serial.print("u2=");
    Serial.println(u2);
}

void loop() {
}
```

The disassembly of the machine code that was generated from the inline assembly code looks like this:

```
mov     r15, r24
mov     r16, r25
add     r15, r15
adc     r16, r16
mov     r24, r15
mov     r25, r16
```

The `lsl` and `rol` instructions are gone! In their place, we now have an `add` and an `adc` instruction. Together, they double the number in `u1`. It turns out that the machine code instruction for `lsl` on a register is the same as that for `add` with the register used twice. The `rol` instruction has been replaced by the `adc` instruction in the same manner. Since we know that `add` and `adc` work with both signed and unsigned numbers, we can easily deduce that `lsl` and `rol` also work with both signed and unsigned numbers.

What about the `lsr` and `ror` instructions? Can they *divide* signed numbers by two? The `lsr` instruction moves all the bits one step to the right, clears bit 7 and moves bit 0 to the Carry Flag. You can use it on a single byte-sized value, or you can use it on the highest byte of a multi-byte value. Remember that we can represent all the numbers from -128 to 127 using one signed byte. Here are the binary numbers that represent the edge cases:

```
-128 = 1000 0000
-1 = 1111 1111
0 = 0000 0000
1 =   0000 0001
127 = 0111 1111
```

As you can see, bit 7 is one for the negative numbers and zero for the positive ones. It's called the **sign bit**, and when the `lsr` instruction clears bit 7 of a negative number, it turns it into a positive one. That's *not* the same thing as dividing by two. We need something else than `lsr` for signed numbers, and the `asr` (**arithmetic shift right**) instruction is the signed replacement for it. The difference is that while the value in bit 7 is still copied to bit 6, it also remains in bit 7. That way, the sign doesn't change, but there's another problem. I'm going to illustrate it with a sketch that runs through all the possible values of a signed byte-sized variable. It uses the `asr` instruction to divide each value by two, and it also prints a comparison using the regular C/C++ division operator.

```
void setup() {
  int8_t i1, i2;

  Serial.begin(9600);
  i1 = -128;
  for ( ; ; )
  {
    asm volatile (
        "mov   r15, %1     \n\t"
        "asr   r15         \n\t"
        "mov   %0, r15     \n\t"
      : "=r" (i2)
      : "r" (i1)
      : "r15"
    );
    Serial.print("asr ");
    Serial.print(i1);
    Serial.print(" = ");
    Serial.print(i2);
    Serial.print(" ... ");
    Serial.print(i1);
    Serial.print(" / 2 = ");
    Serial.println(i1/2);
    if (i1 == 127)
    {
      break;
    }
    i1++;
```

```
    }
}

void loop() {
}
```

Look closely at what's printed, and you'll be able to spot several anomalies:

```
asr -128 = -64 ... -128 / 2 = -64
asr -127 = -64 ... -127 / 2 = -63
asr -126 = -63 ... -126 / 2 = -63
asr -125 = -63 ... -125 / 2 = -62
asr -124 = -62 ... -124 / 2 = -62
.
.
.
asr -5 = -3 ... -5 / 2 = -2
asr -4 = -2 ... -4 / 2 = -2
asr -3 = -2 ... -3 / 2 = -1
asr -2 = -1 ... -2 / 2 = -1
asr -1 = -1 ... -1 / 2 = 0
asr  0 = 0 ...  0 / 2 = 0
asr  1 = 0 ...  1 / 2 = 0
asr  2 = 1 ...  2 / 2 = 1
asr  3 = 1 ...  3 / 2 = 1
asr  4 = 2 ...  4 / 2 = 2
asr  5 = 2 ...  5 / 2 = 2
.
.
.
asr 123 = 61 ... 123 / 2 = 61
asr 124 = 62 ... 124 / 2 = 62
asr 125 = 62 ... 125 / 2 = 62
asr 126 = 63 ... 126 / 2 = 63
asr 127 = 63 ... 127 / 2 = 63
```

Everything looks fine for the positive numbers and the even negative numbers, but the results differ for the odd negative numbers. The C/C++ division operator works uniformly for positive and negative numbers. It performs what is called **integer division**, where the fractional part is discarded. Compare that to the `asr` instruction, which seems to perform integer division on the positive numbers, but rounds the result when dividing negative numbers. It's consistent with a rounding method called **round half down**, or **round half toward negative infinity**. For example, -5 / 2 equals -2.5, which is rounded to -3. With integer division, the quotient would instead be -2, with the fractional part discarded. Look at what the sketch printed, and you'll see these two different results at the -5 line.

Unsigned and Signed Multiplication

There's no division instruction in the AVR instruction set, but there are six different multiplication instructions. I'm going to cover the three basic ones: `mul`, `muls`, and `mulsu`. While the `add` instruction works with both signed and unsigned variables, the multiplication instructions must be correctly matched. This sketch illustrates that:

```
void setup() {
  uint8_t m1 = 0x75, m2 = 0x94;
  uint8_t pul, puh, psl, psh;

  Serial.begin(9600);
  asm volatile (
    "mov   r16, %4     \n\t"
    "mov   r17, %5     \n\t"
    "mul   r16, r17    \n\t"
    "mov   %0, r0      \n\t"
    "mov   %1, r1      \n\t"
    "muls  r16, r17    \n\t"
    "mov   %2, r0      \n\t"
    "mov   %3, r1      \n\t"
    "clr   r1          \n\t"
    : "=r" (pul), "=r" (puh), "=r" (psl), "=r" (psh)
    : "r" (m1), "r" (m2)
    : "r16", "r17"
  );
  Serial.print("pul=");
  Serial.print(pul, HEX);
  Serial.print(" puh=");
  Serial.println(puh, HEX);
```

```
    Serial.print("psl=");
    Serial.print(psl, HEX);
    Serial.print(" psh=");
    Serial.println(psh, HEX);
}

void loop() {
}
```

The output is:

```
pul=A4 puh=43
psl=A4 psh=CE
```
[4]

We begin with two unsigned variables that hold the values 0x75 and 0x94. The assembly code is unaware of the signedness of the variables. 0x75 equals 117, which is the same positive number both as a signed and an unsigned byte-sized variable. 0x94 equals 1001 0100 in binary. If we interpret it as a signed number, it must be negative because the sign bit is set. If we subtract one and invert all the bits, we get 0110 1100 in binary or 0x6c in hexadecimal. The two's complement of 0x6c is 0x94, and 0x94 interpreted as a signed number is -0x6c.

If we multiply the unsigned interpretations of the variables, we get: 0x75 * 0x94 = 0x43a4. In binary, that's 0100 0011 1010 0100.

If we multiply the signed interpretations, we get: 0x75 * -0x6c = -0x315c. 0x315c equals 0011 0001 0101 1100 in binary. The two's complement of that number is 1100 1110 1010 0100, which equals 0xcea4.

As you can see, the signed and unsigned multiplications lead to two different bit patterns. Having a single instruction for both signed and unsigned multiplication won't work.

The output from the sketch shows that the unsigned product is 0x43a4, while the signed product is 0xcea4. That's the same products as we calculated by hand even though the assembly code is unaware of the signedness of the variables. It multiplies the same two variables twice—after copying them to

---

4   The variable names are put together from: p = product, u = unsigned, s = signed, l = lower byte, h = higher byte.

r16 and r17—but using two different multiplication instructions. The unsigned result comes from the `mul` instruction, and the signed result comes from the `muls` instruction. Normally you would use signed variables with the `muls` instruction, but I wanted to show you that the multiplication instructions are entirely unaware of the signedness of the numbers they work with.

There's an important caveat I must mention before we finish our discussion about multiplication. The multiplication instructions put their results in `r0` (the low byte) and `r1` (the high byte). Whenever we trash the zero register, `r1`, we must restore it to zero again. That's what the `clr r1` line does.

The third multiplication instruction is called `mulsu`. It multiplies a signed number with an unsigned number. The signed number must always be in the first operand and the unsigned number in the second operand.

Function Calling Conventions Revisited: Signed 8-bit Return Values

By convention, an 8-bit return value is passed in `r24` regardless of its signedness, and the return value is always extended to 16 bits. Therefore, we must clear the `r25` register for unsigned 8-bit return values. But what about signed 8-bit return values?

Let's extend a signed 8-bit value by prepending an upper byte with zeroes and see what happens. The decimal value -2 equals 0b 1111 1110. With an upper byte of all zeroes, we get 0b 0000 0000 1111 1110, which equals the positive number 254 in decimal. The result we want is the two's complement of 0b 0000 0000 0000 0010, which is 0b 1111 1111 1111 1110. Clearly, we got our first attempt wrong.

We can also try to set all the bits of the upper byte to the same value as the sign bit of the lower byte. Then we get 0b 1111 1111 1111 1110, which is the correct value. The operation we have performed is called **sign extension**.

Here's a snippet of code that performs sign extension for return values:

```
mov    r0, r24
lsl    r0
sbc    r25, r25
```

We move the original 8-bit signed value from r24 to the temporary register, r0. Then we shift r0 one step to the left with the lsl instruction, which moves the most significant bit from r24 to the Carry Flag. The last instruction, sbc, subtracts r25 from itself and then subtracts the Carry Flag from the result. Subtracting r25 from itself clears it, no matter what the original value was. Therefore, we only have two straightforward cases to understand. The first case is when the most significant bit in r24 is zero. Then the Carry Flag is 0, and r25 becomes 0 – 0, which equals 0b 0000 0000. The second case is when the most significant bit in r24 is 1. Then the Carry Flag is 1, and sbc calculates 0 – 1. The result is -1, which equals 0b 1111 1111. In both cases, the most significant bit from r24 is copied to all the bits of the upper byte.

Chapter 16.
More Jumping and Branching

The purpose of this chapter is twofold: to cover more of jumping and branching, and at the same time introduce you to slightly more complex assembly language programs.

A Simple Branch Example

Our first example compares a number to a constant and acts according to the result:

```
uint8_t f(uint8_t input)
{
  uint8_t result;

  asm volatile (
    "mov    r24, %1     \n\t"
    "ldi    r25, 5      \n\t"
    "cp     r24, r25    \n\t"
    "brcs   1f          \n\t"
    "add    r24, r25    \n\t"
```

```
    "1:                   \n\t"
    "mov   %0, r24       \n\t"
    : "=r" (result)
    : "r" (input)
    : "r24", "r25"
  );
  return result;
}

void setup() {
  Serial.begin(9600);
  Serial.println(f(1));
  Serial.println(f(9));
}

void loop() {
}
```

The assembly code copies the content of the `input` variable to the `r24` register. Then, it loads 5 into the `r25` register and executes the `cp` (**compare**) instruction. The `cp` instruction calculates `r24 - r25` and throws away the result, but the SREG flags are affected the same way as they would be by the `sub` instruction.

The Carry Flag is set by `cp` if `r25` is higher than `r24`, and then the `brcs` (**branch if carry set**) instruction branches to label 1. The `r24` register contains the value from the `input` variable at that point, which is then copied to the `result` variable.

The Carry Flag is cleared by `cp` if `r24` is higher than, or equal to, `r25`. In that case, the execution continues on the next line after the `brcs` instruction. The value in `r25` is added to `r24`, and the sum is copied to the `result` variable.

The `f()` function is called twice, with the arguments 1 and 9. The first time, `input` is lower than 5, and therefore it's returned as is. The second time, `input` is higher than 5. The assembly code then returns 9 + 5, which equals 14. Running the sketch, we get the following output:

A Loop Example

This example adds the numbers 0 to 9 with a loop and then subtracts 5 from the sum:

```
void setup() {
  uint8_t result;

  Serial.begin(9600);
  asm volatile (
    "ldi   r24, 0      \n\t"
    "ldi   r25, 0      \n\t"
    "1:                \n\t"
    "cpi   r24, 10     \n\t"
    "brcc 2f           \n\t"
    "add   r25, r24    \n\t"
    "inc   r24         \n\t"
    "rjmp 1b           \n\t"
    "2:                \n\t"
    "subi r25, 5       \n\t"
    "mov  %0, r25      \n\t"
    : "=r" (result)
    :
    : "r24", "r25"
  );
  Serial.print("result=");
  Serial.println(result);
}

void loop() {
}
```

We're using the `r24` register to hold the loop variable, and the `r25` register to hold the sum. Both start at zero. Label 1 is used to continue the loop, and label 2 is used to exit it. The `cpi` (**compare with immediate**) instruction works like the `cp` instruction, except that the second operand is a constant instead of a register. In this case, the `cpi` instruction subtracts 10 from `r24`. The `brcc` (**branch if carry cleared**) instruction continues the execution at label 2 when `r24` reaches 10. As long as `r24` holds a smaller value, `cpi` sets the Carry Flag, and the program adds `r24` (the loop variable) to `r25` (the sum), increments `r24` by one, and jumps back to the `cpi` instruction. The loop adds all the values from 0 to 9, which totals up to 45. When the loop variable in `r24` reaches 10, the execution continues at label 2, and 5 is subtracted from the sum. The subtraction instruction used here is called `subi` (**subtract immediate**) and it subtracts a constant from a register. The final result is 45 – 5, which equals 40, and that is also what the sketch prints:

```
result=40
```

A Switch Example

After a simple branch example and a loop example, it's time for a switch example. We're going to do the assembly equivalent of this C/C++ code:

```
switch (n)
{
  case 0:
    r = 1;
    break;
  case 1:
    r = 2;
    break;
  case 2:
    r = 3;
    break;
  case 3:
    r = 5;
    break;
  default:
    r = 10;
    break;
}
r += 5;
```

The assembly code is in a function called f(), and we're going to test it by passing it the numbers 0 to 4. Here's the sketch:

```
uint8_t f(uint8_t n)
{
  uint8_t r;

  asm volatile (
    "mov   r24, %1    \n\t"
    "cpi   r24, 1     \n\t"
    "breq  2f         \n\t"
    "brcs  1f         \n\t"
    "cpi   r24, 2     \n\t"
    "breq  3f         \n\t"
    "cpi   r24, 3     \n\t"
    "brne  4f         \n\t"
    "ldi   r24, 5     \n\t"
    "rjmp  5f         \n\t"
    "1:               \n\t"
    "ldi   r24, 1     \n\t"
    "rjmp  5f         \n\t"
    "2:               \n\t"
    "ldi   r24, 2     \n\t"
    "rjmp  5f         \n\t"
    "3:               \n\t"
    "ldi   r24, 3     \n\t"
    "rjmp  5f         \n\t"
    "4:               \n\t"
    "ldi   r24, 10    \n\t"
    "5:               \n\t"
    "subi  r24, 0xfb  \n\t"
    "mov   %0, r24    \n\t"
    : "=r" (r)
    : "r" (n)
    : "r24"
  );

  return r;
}

void setup() {
```

```
  uint8_t i;

  Serial.begin(9600);
  for (i=0; i<=4; i++)
  {
    Serial.println(f(i));
  }
}

void loop() {
}
```

The breq (**branch if equal**) instruction branches if the two operands to the cpi instruction on the line above are equal. The brne (**branch if not equal**) instruction branches if they are *not* equal.

There's a rather strange line close to the end of the assembly code:

```
subi r24, 0xfb
```

Since the C/C++ code contains an addition, we would expect an addition—not a subtraction. The problem is that there's no addi instruction in AVR assembly. There's an adiw instruction that adds a constant to a word (a register pair), and there's an add instruction that adds two registers, but no addi instruction that adds a constant to a single register. Remember that B − C equals B plus the two's complement of C. If we want to add 5, we can instead subtract the number that 5 is the two's complement of. 5 equals 0000 0101 in binary. Subtract 1, and we get 0000 0100. Invert the bits, and we get 1111 1011, which is the same as 0xfb. The two's complement of 0xfb is 5, and subtracting 0xfb is the same as adding the two's complement—that is—adding 5. So instead of adding 5, we can subtract 0xfb.

Analyze the program line by line and try to figure out how it works. I suggest that you print it on paper, or make a copy on paper, and write notes at the end of every line. Perhaps you can better visualize the jumps and branches if you draw arrows to the target lines. Try to figure out what the sketch prints without looking at the C/C++ code. The correct answer is in the footnote below.[5]

---

[5] The sketch prints the numbers: 6, 7, 8, 10, and 15.

A Branch Table Example

We're going to do the assembly equivalent of this C/C++ code once more:

```
switch (n)
{
  case 0:
    r = 1;
    break;
  case 1:
    r = 2;
    break;
  case 2:
    r = 3;
    break;
  case 3:
    r = 5;
    break;
  default:
    r = 10;
    break;
}
r += 5;
```

This time the solution involves something called a branch table. As usual, we start by having a look at the sketch:

```
uint8_t f(uint8_t n)
{
  uint8_t r;

  asm volatile (
    "mov   r24, %1          \n\t"
    "cpi   r24, 4           \n\t"
    "brsh  6f               \n\t"
    "ldi   zl, pm_lo8(1f)   \n\t"
    "ldi   zh, pm_hi8(1f)   \n\t"
    "add   zl, r24          \n\t"
    "adc   zh, r1           \n\t"
    #ifdef __AVR_HAVE_EIJMP_EICALL__
    "ldi   r25, pm_hh8(1f)  \n\t"
```

```
        "adc   r25, r1           \n\t"
        "out   0x3c, r25         \n\t"
        "eijmp                   \n\t"
        #else
        "ijmp                    \n\t"
        #endif
        "1:                      \n\t"
        "rjmp 2f                 \n\t"
        "rjmp 3f                 \n\t"
        "rjmp 4f                 \n\t"
        "rjmp 5f                 \n\t"
        "2:                      \n\t"
        "ldi   r24, 1            \n\t"
        "rjmp 7f                 \n\t"
        "3:                      \n\t"
        "ldi   r24, 2            \n\t"
        "rjmp 7f                 \n\t"
         "4:                     \n\t"
        "ldi   r24, 3            \n\t"
        "rjmp 7f                 \n\t"
        "5:                      \n\t"
        "ldi   r24, 5            \n\t"
        "rjmp 7f                 \n\t"
        "6:                      \n\t"
        "ldi   r24, 10           \n\t"
        "7:                      \n\t"
        "subi r24, 0xfb          \n\t"
        "mov   %0, r24           \n\t"
        : "=r" (r)
        : "r" (n)
        : "r24", "r25"
    );

    return r;
}

void setup() {
    uint8_t i;

    Serial.begin(9600);
    for (i=0; i<=4; i++)
```

```
  {
    Serial.println(f(i));
  }
}

void loop() {
}
```

The first lines take the control variable (the n variable in the C/C++ code) and check if it's higher than 3, which is the highest case value:

```
"mov   r24, %1        \n\t"
"cpi   r24, 4         \n\t"
"brsh  6f             \n\t"
```

A higher value means that the execution should continue at the default case, which has the label 6. The brsh (**branch if same or higher**) instruction branches if the first operand to the cpi instruction is equal to or higher than the second operand. If the control variable holds a value lower than 4, the program continues with this intriguing section of code instead of branching:

```
"ldi   zl, pm_lo8(1f)  \n\t"
"ldi   zh, pm_hi8(1f)  \n\t"
"add   zl, r24         \n\t"
"adc   zh, r1          \n\t"
#ifdef __AVR_HAVE_EIJMP_EICALL__
"ldi   r25, pm_hh8(1f) \n\t"
"adc   r25, r1         \n\t"
"out   0x3c, r25       \n\t"
"eijmp                 \n\t"
#else
"ijmp                  \n\t"
#endif
"1:                    \n\t"
"rjmp  2f              \n\t"
"rjmp  3f              \n\t"
"rjmp  4f              \n\t"
"rjmp  5f              \n\t"
```

The **modifiers** `pm_lo8()` and `pm_hi8()` extract the low and high bytes of a program memory address. The first two lines use them to load the low and high bytes of the address of label 1 into the `zl` and `zh` registers. After these two lines, the z register points to the **branch table**, or **jump table**, which consists of four `rjmp` instructions in a row. The next line adds the control variable in `r24` to the `zl` register. By adding the zero register, `r1`, to the `zh` register using the `adc` instruction, a possible carry from the addition of `r24` and `zl` is transferred to the `zh` register.

The Arduino Uno has 32 KB of flash program memory, while the Arduino Mega 2560 has 256 KB. If we use the z register to store the branch table address, we can only reach the first $2 * 2^{16} = 128$ KB of program memory. That's fine on the Uno, but on the Mega 2560, we can't reach the upper half of the program memory that way. To solve this problem, the ATmega2560 microcontroller in the Arduino Mega 2560 has two additional instructions called `eicall` and `eijmp`. The line `#ifdef __AVR_HAVE_EIJMP_EICALL__` is there to allow two versions of the code: one for the Mega 2560, and one for the Uno. The Mega 2560 lines look like this:

```
"ldi    r25, pm_hh8(1f)  \n\t"
"adc    r25, r1          \n\t"
"out    0x3c, r25        \n\t"
"eijmp                   \n\t"
```

The modifier `pm_hh8()` extracts the bits 16 to 23 from a program memory address. The first line uses it to load that part of the branch table address into `r25`. Next, we add the zero register to `r25` using the `adc` instruction. If there's a carry from the earlier addition of `zh` and `r1`, it will be transferred to `r25`. We can't store the byte from `r25` in the z register, because z is only 16 bits wide. The ATmega2560 microcontroller solves that problem by introducing a new I/O register called EIND (**extended indirect register**). We output `r25` to it at I/O address 0x3c. Finally, we use the instruction `eijmp` (**extended indirect jump**) to jump to the address held by the EIND and z registers.

When you run the program on the Uno there's no EIND register, and the only line needed for the jump is this one:

```
"ijmp                   \n\t"
```

The `ijmp` (**indirect jump**) instruction jumps to the address held by the z register alone.

The branch table consists of these lines:

```
"1:                     \n\t"
"rjmp 2f                \n\t"
"rjmp 3f                \n\t"
"rjmp 4f                \n\t"
"rjmp 5f                \n\t"
```

Using the control variable to index the table works because the `rjmp` instructions are 16 bits wide, and the addresses supplied to the `eijmp` and `ijmp` instructions are program memory addresses, which address 16-bit word locations. Each `rjmp` instruction points to the code following the corresponding case statement. By now, you should be able to figure out how the rest of the program works by yourself.

An Empty Sketch and a Delay Subroutine

Remarkably, we can work with a completely blank sketch where we have deleted everything that the Arduino IDE puts there by default. It shouldn't even have empty `setup()` and `loop()` functions—we delete *everything* from the `.ino` file. Then we add an `.S` file to hold the assembly code. In our next example, the `.S` file looks like this:

```
.global main

delay_sub:
    ldi   r16, 255
    ldi   r17, 255
    ldi   r18, 20
delay_loop:
    dec   r16
    brne  delay_loop
    dec   r17
```

```
        brne  delay_loop
        dec   r18
        brne  delay_loop
        ret

main:
   sbi    0x04, 5
blink:
   sbi    0x05, 5
   call   delay_sub
   cbi    0x05, 5
   call   delay_sub
   rjmp   blink
```

The .global directive makes the symbol main visible to the linker. Without setup() and loop() functions, the Arduino starts executing the code at the main label first.

Our goal is to blink the debug LED. To set bit 5 in the DDRB register, we use:

```
sbi    0x04, 5
```

The loop that follows sets and clears bit 5 in the PORTB register indefinitely, with a delay after each change.

The delay_sub subroutine consists of three nested loops, each using the brne instruction. In our previous encounter with it, it was positioned after a compare instruction. There, it branched if the two operands weren't equal. What the brne instruction really does is branch if the Zero Flag is cleared. Comparing two operands with different values clears the Zero Flag because comparing is the same as subtracting and throwing away the result. Two different values have a non-zero difference.

The inner loop uses the r16 register to count down from 255 to 0. As long as the result is non-zero, the brne instruction makes the loop continue. When r16 reaches 0, r17 is decremented by 1. Then the inner loop starts again, with r16 wrapping around from 0 to 255. When r16 reaches 0 the next time, r17 is once more decremented by 1, and so on. When r17 finally reaches 0, the outer loop runs a single turn, decrementing r18 by one. Then everything starts over again with the inner loop. It's not until the outer loop ends, because `r18` reaches zero, that the `delay_sub` subroutine returns. All this iterating takes time, and I've picked initial values for each loop that make the total delay suitable for blinking the debug LED.

Chapter 17.
Memory Clobbering

Here's a sketch that doesn't work quite as expected:

```
uint8_t u;
uint8_t *p;

void setup() {
  uint8_t i;

  Serial.begin(9600);
  u = 0x88;
  p = &u;
  for (i=0; i<100; i++)
  {
    u += i;
  }
  asm volatile (
    "ldi   r16, 0x99 \n\t"
    "st    %a0, r16  \n\t"
    :
    : "e" (p)
    : "r16"
```

```
  );
  for (i=0; i<100; i++)
  {
     u += i;
  }
  Serial.println(u);
}

void loop() {
}
```

The asm statement receives a pointer, p, to a uint8_t variable, u. The two loops are only there to make the compiler optimize the code in a particular way, and I'll explain why later. The e constraint tells the compiler to use a pointer register pair for the input operand. The st (**store indirect from register to data space**) instruction copies the value 0x99 from the r16 register to the memory location pointed to by p. The operand %a0 resembles %A0, but mixing them up would be a big mistake because %a0 represents the whole pointer register pair. The sketch outputs 52, but it should output 239 (you will see the correct version do that later). The disassembly reveals the problem:

```
ldi     r18, 0x88
ldi     r24, 0x00
52e:
add     r18, r24
subi    r24, 0xFF
cpi     r24, 0x64       ; 100
brne    .-8             ; 0x52e
ldi     r30, 0x16
ldi     r31, 0x01
ldi     r16, 0x99
st      Z, r16
ldi     r24, 0x00
540:
add     r18, r24
subi    r24, 0xFF
cpi     r24, 0x64       ; 100
brne    .-8             ; 0x540
sts     0x0116, r18
```

The u variable is stored in r18 and the i variable in r24. The first loop consists of these lines:

```
52e:
add     r18, r24
subi    r24, 0xFF
cpi     r24, 0x64       ; 100
brne    .-8             ; 0x52e
```

When the loop ends, r18 still represents the u variable, and now it holds the sum. The lines from the asm statement come next:

```
ldi     r30, 0x16
ldi     r31, 0x01
ldi     r16, 0x99
st      Z, r16
```

The first two lines copy the address from the pointer p to the r30 and r31 registers. They are the lower and upper bytes of the z register. That's the pointer register pair the compiler picked when it saw the e constraint. Next, 0x99 is copied into the address pointed to by z. Since z holds the same value as p, and p points to u, it follows that u *should* now be 0x99. What happens next comes as a bit of a surprise:

```
ldi     r24, 0x00
540:
add     r18, r24
subi    r24, 0xFF
cpi     r24, 0x64       ; 100
brne    .-8             ; 0x540
```

The i variable is still stored in r24, and it's now cleared as we would expect. But then the second loop starts, and it still uses the r18 register to store the u variable. The compiler is unaware of the fact that we've used a pointer to change the value of u inside the asm statement. It tries to optimize the generated code by using a register to represent u in the loops. That's clever, but what happens next ruins it:

```
sts        0x0116, r18
```

When the second loop ends, the version of u that's stored in r18 is copied to the memory location that held the version of u that the asm statement worked with. We've been working with two different u variables in parallel without knowing it, and the sketch outputs the wrong result. As I've explained before, the compiler doesn't know what goes on inside the asm statements unless we tell it. Let's tell it, and see what happens. We keep everything in the sketch as is, except we add "memory" to the clobber list, like so:

```
asm volatile (
   "ldi   r16, 0x99 \n\t"
   "st    %a0, r16   \n\t"
   :
   : "e" (p)
   : "r16", "memory"
);
```

The sketch outputs 239 instead of 52. That's the correct result, and the disassembly now looks like this:

```
ldi        r25, 0x88
ldi        r24, 0x00
52e:
add        r25, r24
subi       r24, 0xFF
cpi        r24, 0x64       ; 100
brne       .-8             ; 0x52e
sts        0x0116, r25
ldi        r30, 0x16
ldi        r31, 0x01
ldi        r16, 0x99
st         Z, r16
lds        r18, 0x0116
ldi        r24, 0x00
548:
add        r18, r24
subi       r24, 0xFF
cpi        r24, 0x64       ; 100
brne       .-8             ; 0x548
```

```
sts     0x0116, r18
```

This version is pretty similar to the first one, but there are a few crucial differences. The `u` variable is still held in a register, `r25`, during the first loop. The first significant difference comes when the loop ends. Then the `r25` register is copied to the memory location that holds the `u` variable. Next, the `asm` statement runs and overwrites it. That's precisely what was supposed to happen—not because it's a logical thing to do—but because it's how the sketch is supposed to work. Before the second loop starts, the `u` variable stored in memory is copied to the `r18` register. The loop runs, using `r18`, and then the sum from `r18` is copied back to the `u` variable memory location.

All the extra copying isn't ideal from an optimization point of view, but it's necessary to avoid the kind of bug we encountered in our first version of the sketch. The "`memory`" clobber tells the compiler that the `asm` statement reads from or writes to memory in ways that aren't listed in the input and output operands. That makes the compiler copy values held temporarily in registers back to memory before the `asm` statement runs, and also copy values from memory back to temporary registers after the `asm` statement is finished.

Chapter 18.
Assembly Files Revisited

Assembly Files and Preprocessing

An assembly file can have an upper case .S extension or a lower case .s extension. The difference between them is that a file with an upper case extension is sent through the C preprocessor before the assembly stage. The Arduino IDE doesn't support the lower case extension even though the GCC compiler it uses does. That no loss in practice, because we can do many useful things with the aid of the preprocessor. There's also an extension called .sx that's equivalent to the .S extension, but it doesn't work either with the Arduino IDE.

Using Macro Substitutions

This is the third time we study a sketch that utilizes a timer and interrupts to blink the debug LED. The C/C++ part of the Arduino sketch is the same as before:

```
extern "C" {
  void prepare();
  void __vector_13();
}

void setup() {
  prepare();
}

void loop() {
}
```

The .S file for our third version of the sketch looks like this:

```
.global __vector_13
.global prepare

// Constants
#define __zero_reg__    1
#define __SREG__        0x3f
#define DEBUG_LED       0b00100000
#define PORTB_IO        0x05

// Registers
#define mask            r16
#define value           r17
#define temp            r18

__vector_13:

    push mask
    push value
    in   temp, __SREG__
    push temp

    ldi  mask, DEBUG_LED
    in   value, PORTB_IO
    eor  value, mask
    out  PORTB_IO, value
```

```
    pop     temp
    out     __SREG__, temp
    pop     value
    pop     mask

    reti

prepare:

    ldi     r18, 0b00100000
    out     0x04, r18

    ldi     xl, 0x80
    ldi     xh, 0x00

    st      x+, __zero_reg__
    ldi     r18, 2
    st      x+, r18
    st      x, __zero_reg__

    ldi     xl, 0x6f
    ldi     xh, 0x00
    ldi     r18, 1
    st      x, r18

    ret
```

Everything works as before, but this time I've used macro substitution with #define to remove some of the magic numbers from the __vector_13 part of the assembly code. As a comparison, I've kept the prepare part of the sketch as is. A less obvious use of #define is to move the register names out of the assembly code too, as these lines help with:

```
#define mask           r16
#define value          r17
#define temp           r18
```

If you decide to use another register, you can change it at a single location. There's no need to use this method if your assembly code is short, but you might find it useful if the code is a bit longer.

Chapter 19.
Inline Assembly or Assembly Files

You can add assembly code to your sketches in two different ways: with inline assembly, or with assembly files.

Programming in inline assembly is pretty error-prone. I've shown you several times throughout the book how you can easily shoot yourself in the foot with inline assembly. Still, it can be convenient to write a block of inline assembly code under the right circumstances, depending on what particular task you have at hand. Inline assembly works best for small blocks of code that you want to embed in C/C++ functions.

If you use assembly files instead, you define functions in an .S file and add it to your sketch. A function call takes 4 to 5 clock cycles, so it might be better to use inline assembly if you must save clock cycles for some reason. You must follow the correct function calling conventions when you accept calls from C/C++ code to your assembly functions. That can also be a bit error-prone, but usually much less so than programming in inline assembly. Assembly files work best when you need more than a small block of assembly code, and the result usually looks much cleaner than inline assembly code.

Appendix A.
Disassembling a Compiled Sketch

On macOS

Before we can disassemble a compiled sketch, we must figure out where it is. The easiest way is to let the Arduino IDE tell us. Click on Arduino in the menu bar and select Preferences. Look for a setting called "Show verbose output during" and mark the "compilation" checkbox. Finish by clicking OK.

The next time you upload a sketch, you will see more information than usual. One of the last lines should start with:

/Applications/Arduino.app/Contents/Java/hardware/tools/avr/bin/avr-size -A

The rest of the line will look somewhat different for each new sketch, but it should be something like this:

/var/folders/nt/0bzbl86x751f78kt0jwkmvtc0000gn/T/arduino_build_508743/sketchname.ino.elf

To perform the actual disassembly, we use a tool called `avr-objdump`. You run it like so:

```
/Applications/Arduino.app/Contents/Java/hardware/tools/avr/bin/avr-objdump -d
```

Supply it with the pathname of the `.elf` file that you got from the Arduino IDE.

On Windows

Before we can disassemble a compiled sketch, we must figure out where it is. The easiest way is to let the Arduino IDE tell us. Click on File in the menu bar and select Preferences. Look for a setting called "Show verbose output during" and mark the "compilation" checkbox. Finish by clicking OK.

The next time you upload a sketch, you will see more information than usual. One of the last lines should start with:

```
"C:\\Program Files (x86)\\Arduino\\hardware\\tools\\avr/bin/avr-size" -A
```

The rest of the line will look somewhat different for each new sketch, but it should be something like this:

```
"C:\\Users\\youraccount\\AppData\\Local\\Temp\\arduino_build_624859/sketchname.ino.elf"
```

To perform the actual disassembly, we use a tool called `avr-objdump`. You run it like so:

```
C:\"Program Files (x86)"\Arduino\hardware\tools\avr\bin\avr-objdump -d
```

Supply it with the pathname of the `.elf` file that you got from the Arduino IDE.

Appendix B.
Where to Find More Information

Basic Asm Statements
https://gcc.gnu.org/onlinedocs/gcc/Basic-Asm.html

Extended Asm Statements
https://gcc.gnu.org/onlinedocs/gcc/Extended-Asm.html

Constraints
https://gcc.gnu.org/onlinedocs/gcc/Constraints.html

Explicit Register Variables
https://gcc.gnu.org/onlinedocs/gcc/Explicit-Register-Variables.html

Inline Assembler Cookbook
https://www.nongnu.org/avr-libc/user-manual/inline_asm.html

What registers are used by the C compiler?
https://www.microchip.com/webdoc/AVRLibcReferenceManual/FAQ_1faq_reg_usage.html

AVR Function Attributes
https://gcc.gnu.org/onlinedocs/gcc/AVR-Function-Attributes.html

ATmega328P Datasheet
http://ww1.microchip.com/downloads/en/DeviceDoc/Atmel-7810-Automotive-Microcontrollers-ATmega328P_Datasheet.pdf

Atmel ATmega640/V-1280/V-1281/V-2560/V-2561/V Datasheet
https://ww1.microchip.com/downloads/en/devicedoc/atmel-2549-8-bit-avr-microcontroller-atmega640-1280-1281-2560-2561_datasheet.pdf

AVR Options
https://gcc.gnu.org/onlinedocs/gcc/AVR-Options.html

Relocatable Expression Modifiers
https://sourceware.org/binutils/docs/as/AVR_002dModifiers.html

AVR Assembler
https://www.microchip.com/webdoc/avrassembler/

GCC Inline Assembly HOWTO
https://www.ibiblio.org/gferg/ldp/GCC-Inline-Assembly-HOWTO.html

Common Function Attributes
https://gcc.gnu.org/onlinedocs/gcc/Common-Function-Attributes.html

The GNU Assembler Labels
http://tigcc.ticalc.org/doc/gnuasm.html#SEC46

Interrupts
```
https://www.nongnu.org/avr-libc/user-manual/
group__avr__interrupts.html
```

Special Function Registers
```
https://www.nongnu.org/avr-libc/user-manual/
group__avr__sfr__notes.html
```

AVR Intruction Set Manual
```
http://ww1.microchip.com/downloads/en/devicedoc/
atmel-0856-avr-instruction-set-manual.pdf
```

Reasons you should NOT use inline asm
```
https://gcc.gnu.org/wiki/DontUseInlineAsm
```

Index

1
16-bit addition	108
16-bit opcodes	37

3
32-bit opcodes	37

A
adc	108
add	11
add with carry	108
and	83
andi	83
arguments	75
arithmetic shift right	86, 110, 112
asl	110
asr	86, 110, 112
assembler template	15
assembly file	95, 139, 143
ATmega2560	9
ATmega328P	9

B
b (backward)	48
basic asm statement	19, 80
baud rate	14
bitmask	83
blank sketch	129
borrow	109
branch table	128
branching instructions	49
brcc	122
brcs	120
breq	124
brlo	50
brne	124
brsh	127

C
C preprocessor	139
C stub function	65
call	61
call-saved registers	80
call-used registers	17, 80
carry	41
Carry Flag	40, 84, 86
cbi	26
CISC	9
clear	83
cleared	41
cli	91
clobber	17
clobber list	16
collision	80
com	83
Complex Instruction Set Computer	9
conditional	49
constants	30
constraint	29
constraint a	30
constraint d	30
constraint e	134
constraint modifier	29
constraint r	29
correct constraint	51
cp	50, 120
cpi	121
CPU core	9

D
Data Direction Register B	24
data space	10

datasheets	10
DDB5	31
DDRB	24
DDRB constant	31
debug LED	21, 23
dec	100
delay()	22
destination	36
destination register	11
digitalWrite	23
disassemble	6
disassemble a compiled sketch	145, 146
disassembler	6
divide signed numbers by two	111
divides by two	86
double a 16-bit number	85
double a 32-bit number	85
DRAM	10
duplicates of inline assembly code	48
Dynamic RAM	10

E

earlyclobber operands	78
EEPROM	10
eicall	128
eijmp	128
EIND	128
Electrically Erasable Programmable Read-Only Memory	10
empty sketch	129
eor	83
even-numbered registers	61
execute	4
extend 8-bit return values	68
extended asm statement	19, 67, 80
extended I/O registers	10
extended indirect jump	128
extended indirect register	128
extern "C"	22

F

f (forward)	48
file-level basic asm statement	67
fixed registers	17
flags	38
flash program memory	10
free to use any call-used register	80
function call	143
function calling convention	61, 67
function epilogue	75
function parameters	80
function prologue	75

G

general-purpose registers	10
Global Interrupt Enable	91
global interrupt flag	91
global variables	99
goto	47

H

Harvard architecture	10

I

I/O registers	10
I/O space	25
ijmp	129
inc	100
indirect jump	129
inline assembly	14, 143
input operands	16
instruction	5
instruction encoded	37
instruction set manual	36
instruction set nomenclature	36
integer division	113
intermediate	75
interrupt	87
interrupt handler	87
interrupt routine	87
interrupt service routine	87
interrupt vector	89
interrupt vector names	93
inverse	83
ISR (Interrupt Service Routine) macro	92

ISR_BLOCK	93
ISR_NAKED	92
ISR_NOBLOCK	93

J

jmp	47
jump table	128
jumping	47

L

labels	6, 48
Last In First Out	53
ld	44
ldi	23
lds	100
leaky abstractions	6
LIFO	53
little-endian	38
local variables	72, 80
logic instructions	83
logical shift left	84
logical shift right	86
lsl	84, 110
lsr	86

M

machine code	3
macro substitution	141
magic numbers	30
main	130
mask	83
memory clobbering	133, 137
microcontroller	9
modifiers	128
mov	16
mul	114, 116
muls	114, 116
mulsu	114, 116
multiple copies of the same label	48
multiplies numbers by two	84

N

naked attribute	68, 80

neg	102, 104
nested interrupts	91
nested loops	130
newline-tab-sequence	15
nop	19
not	83
number and a colon	48

O

one's complement	83
opcodes	4
operand order	11
operands	11
optimizing	6, 61
or	83
order of operands	11
ori	83
out	24
output operands	15
overflow	105
Overflow Interrupt Enable bit	89

P

parameters	75
PB5	31
PC	37
peripheral features	9
pinMode	23
pm_hh8()	128
pm_hi8()	128
pm_lo8()	128
pointer register pairs	43
pop	53, 57
port B	24
port D	24
PORTB	24
PORTB5	32
ports	24
post-increment	45
pre-decrement	45
Program Counter	37
pure assembly function	80, 81
push	53, 57

Index | **153**

Q
qualifier   15

R
r1   18, 91
r18-r27 and r30-r31   80
r2-r17 and r28-r29   80
r27:r26   43
r29:r28   43
r31:r30   43
RAMEND   57
random()   60
Rd   36
Reduced Instruction Set Computer   9
register file   10
registers   10
relative jump   48
ret   61
reti   91
return address   61
reverse engineering   6
RISC   9
rjmp   48
rol   84, 110
ror   86
rotate left through carry   84
rotate right through carry   86
rotating   84
round half down   114
round half toward negative infinity   114
Rr   36

S
save and restore   81
sbc   108, 109
sbi   26
sei   91
serial monitor   14
Serial.begin()   14
Serial.print()   14
Serial.println()   14
set   41, 83
SFR   31

sign bit   112
sign extension   116
signed 8-bit return values   116
signedness   101
simple constraint   29
simple upper registers   30
source   36
source register   11
Special Function Registers   31
SPH   55
SPL   55
SRAM   10
SREG   38
st   134
stack   53
stack pointer   55, 57
Static RAM   10
status register   38
sts   24
sub   108
subi   122
subroutine   66
subtract with carry   109

T
temporary storage   75
Timer/Counter 1   89
TIMER1 OVF   89
TIMER1_OVF_vect   92
TIMSK1   89
toggle   84
two's complement   101
Two's Complement Overflow Flag   105

U
upper registers   30

V
volatile   15, 19, 100
von Neumann architecture   10

X
x   43

x+	45
xor	83

Y

y	43
y pointer register pair	72

Z

z	43
zero register	18, 91

_

__attribute__((noinline))	59
__attribute__((used))	22, 100
__AVR_HAVE_EIJMP_EICALL__	128
__SREG__	39
_SFR_IO_ADDR()	31

-

-x	45

.

.global directive	90, 130
.s extension	96, 139
.S file	129
.sx	139

\

\n\t	15

&

& constraint modifier	80

#

#define	141

%

%0	15
%a0	134
%A4	33

=

=	29

Printed in Great Britain
by Amazon